The Strategos Guide to
Value Stream &
Process Mapping

Copyright 2006 Strategos, Inc.

Published by

Enna Products Corporation

1602 Carolina St.
Unit B-3
Bellingham, WA 98229
Fax: 905 481 0756
E-mail: info@enna.com

Copyright 2007 Book Cover, Enna Products Corporation

Published simultaneously in Canada

Manufactured in the United States of America

International Standard Book Number: 1-897363-43-5

Library of Congress Catalog Card Number: 2007923999

First Printing: February 2007

07   07   07   3   2   1

Distributed by Productivity Press, an imprint of CRC Press
711 Third Avenue, New York, NY 10017
2 Park Square, Milton Park, Abingdon, Oxon OX14 4RN
www.productivitypress.com

CRC Press is an imprint of the Taylor & Francis Group, an informa business

Adapted from Quarterman Lee's *The Strategos Guide to Value Stream and Process Mapping,* 2006, Strategos Inc.

Enna Products Corporation

1602 Carolina St.
Unit B-3
Bellingham, WA 98229

Published by Enna Products Corporation

www.enna.com

Publisher's Note

Welcome to Enna's first edition *Value Stream & Process Mapping Guide*. Between these two covers, author Quarterman Lee taps his vast experience and expertise to make Process and Value Stream Mapping a simple and painless process. Quarterman has more than 20 years experience in teaching Lean manufacturing principles and helping clients improve their businesses and manufacturing operations; it is a pleasure to publish his knowledge and wisdom.

While Process Mapping has its roots in the late Industrial Revolution, and Value Stream Mapping is forever linked to Taiichi Ohno's Toyota Production System, there is a need to provide a link between these two systems to provide relevance to today's business needs. In fact, with the expansion of the global marketplace and emerging economies this book brings clarity to these Lean techniques. Quarterman begins with a general introduction to the topic at hand and divides the concepts into easily manageable sections. From there, he leads the reader through Process Mapping Techniques from start to finish, present to future. Value Stream Mapping is covered with an equally in-depth analysis that not only explains the virtues of the system, but also acknowledges when it is *not* necessary. These chapters feature valuable sections with tips for facilitators and planning sessions. The final chapters focus on combining these systems with Lean concepts and manufacturing strategy. Last but not least, Quarterman emphasizes the importance of the human aspect of these systems.

German philosopher and novelist Johann Wolfgang Goethe once remarked that, "Knowing is not enough; we must apply!" We here at Enna couldn't agree more; our slogan *Knowledge into Practice* reflects that same spirit of action. We hope you enjoy our publication of Quarterman's experience and knowledge. We always welcome comments and suggestions from our audience; please send us an e-mail at info@enna.com. If you are looking for more in depth material on VSM or other Lean principles, visit us at www.enna.com and view our entire range of Training Packages.

Sincerely,

Collin Mcloughlin
President

Author's Preface

 With the recent publicity about Value Stream Mapping, many seem to imagine that it is another magical answer for all manufacturing problems. In this book, I have tried to take a realistic point of view, recognizing the benefits as well as the limitations to mapping.

This book acquaints the reader with Process Mapping as well as Value Stream Mapping. It thereby provides a dual set of tools. This dual set is far more effective than either technique alone.

The mechanics of mapping techniques are not all that difficult. The important question is "What to do with it" rather than "How to do it." To answer the first question, we explore some of the issues of Manufacturing Strategy and Lean Manufacturing Strategy. Mapping only portrays and highlights workflow and certain other aspects of a manufacturing system. Equally important but often overlooked are the human aspects—the "socio" side of these highly complex socio-technical systems. While we introduce certain aspects of these related issues, it would be impossible to cover them thoroughly in a single work.

I have attempted to provide a practical, step-by-step framework for mapping that leads the reader through a mapping project in a systematic way. Finally, we attempt to identify and impart related skills, such as facilitation, that practitioners need in order to realize the full potential of these powerful techniques.

I hope you find this book useful and valuable. Comments from readers are always welcome.

Best regards,

Quarterman Lee

The Strategos Guide to
Value Stream & Process Mapping

Table of Contents

List of Figures

List of Tables

Chapter

1.0 Introduction

Value Stream Mapping and Process Mapping are techniques that help to visualize work processes. By doing so, they enable improvement teams and managers to identify areas for streamlining the work, reducing defects and improving operations in many ways. Both techniques are valuable tools for Lean Manufacturing.

Process Mapping—Was pioneered by Frank Gilbreth in the early 1900's. It is effective across a wide range of situations and levels of detail. Process mapping is fundamental. It assumes no pre-conceived set of arrangements, tools or technique. Figure 1 shows a typical Process Map.

Value Stream Mapping—is a more recent technique designed specifically around the Toyota version of Lean Manufacturing. Figure 2 illustrates this technique.

These two approaches view the same work from different perspectives and on different levels. Each has a place in the improvement of work processes and the attainment of business goals.

A factory is enormously complex. Only visuals convey enough information to understand the pieces, relationships, the hidden wastes and time-domain behaviors. Visualization brings a deep understanding and leads to major breakthroughs in productivity and other performance. It leads to consensus on systemic problems and remedies.

While a finished process or value stream map communicates valuable information, the most important benefit comes from its creation. During the mapping process, when properly done, insights grow, paradigms shift and consensus builds. Not only does mapping lead to better processes, it leads to a consensus that enables and enhances implementation.

Mapping of work processes is analogous to geographic mapping in many ways (hence the term). Both geographic and work maps tell us:

- **Where We Are**
- **Where We Want to Go**
- **How to Get There**
- **Difficulties Along the Way**

Process and Value Stream Maps tell us where we are by documenting how the current process performs work. They tell us where we want to go by helping to define a process that is speedy and economically efficient (the ideal state map). They help to guide us towards the ideal future state and, they can identify difficulties to overcome. *Ultimately, the goals of Process and Value Stream Mapping are to eliminate waste and to support marketing and business strategies.*

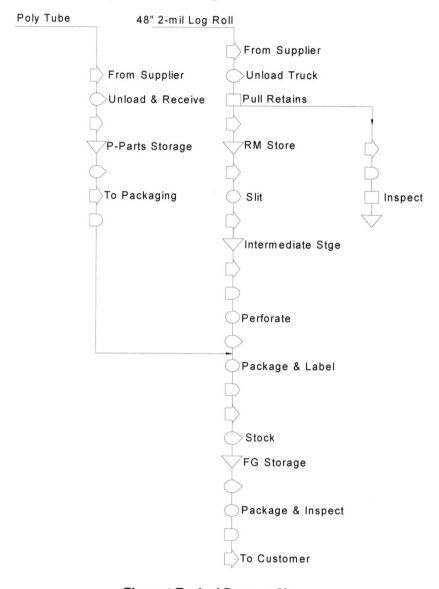

Figure 1 Typical Process Map

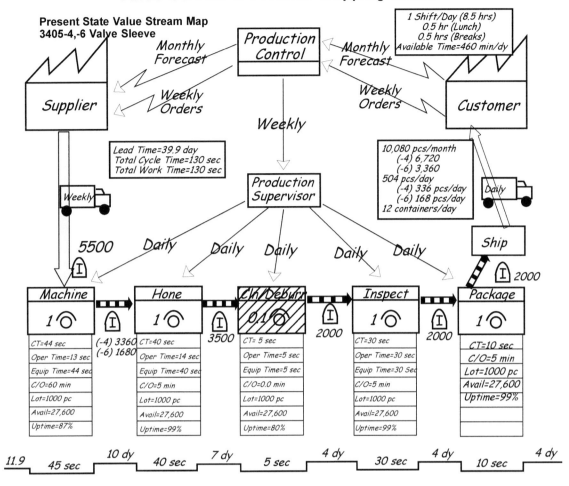

Figure 2 Typical Value Stream Map

Types of Maps

Figures 1 and 2 appear quite different just as many geographic maps have quite different appearances. Like geographic maps, work maps come in many forms; each suited for different situations and different purposes. Maps also vary in their level of detail, again, depending on their purpose. For example, we often use one map for cross-country driving and a second map to find our way to a specific address in the city of our arrival. Figure 3 is a street map near Kansas City. It shows interstate highways, primary feeder roads and a few other large-scale features visible to the motorist. This would be a very useful map for a driver traveling to Kansas City International Airport. However, it would be less helpful if the same motorist were driving to a specific address on 107th Street since 107th Street does not even show at this level of detail.

The road map of figure 3 has limited use for a pilot who might also be traveling to Kansas City International Airport. Pilots might discern the general pattern of roads from the air but they cannot see street signs that identify specific roads. Nor does this map inform them of radio and radio navigation frequencies. It does not display the boundaries of controlled airspace.

Figure 4 is an aviation chart for the same area. It shows features that are visible from the air and does not show features that are only identifiable from the ground. It shows the location of navigation beacons, tall obstructions, airspace boundaries and even minor airports with grass runways (useful in an emergency). An aviation map has little use for the motorist. There is no detail about streets and no way to orient the motorist with respect to street signs or ground level landmarks.

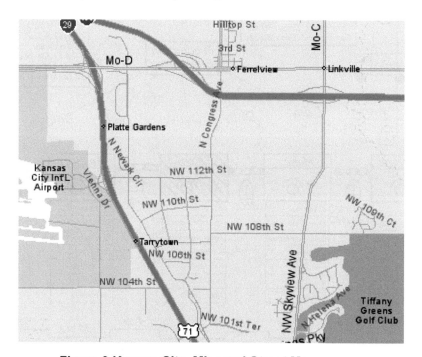

Figure 3 Kansas City, Missouri Street Map

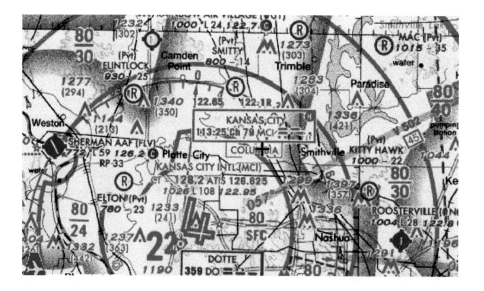

Figure 4 Aviation Chart of the Same Area

The key point is this: select a map and its level of detail that fits your specific purpose. There is no all-purpose mapping technique for analyzing work processes or for navigation.

Maps have varying degrees of accuracy. Figure 5 shows the map that Lewis and Clark used for their exploration of North America in 1803. This is hardly an accurate representation but it was they best available and undoubtedly useful. Indeed, one purpose of the expedition was to improve the accuracy of available maps.

"The map is not the territory"
--Alfred Korzybski

This means that an abstraction derived from something, or a reaction to it, is not the thing itself, e.g., the pain from a stone falling on your foot is not the stone; one's opinion of another person is not that person; **a metaphorical representation of a concept is not the concept itself.**

A specific abstraction or reaction does not capture all facets of its source — e.g., the pain in your foot does not convey the internal structure of the stone. This may limit an individual's understanding and cognition unless the two are distinguished.

Maps need not be completely accurate to be useful. The important point for the users of maps is to be aware of the possible inaccuracies and work accordingly. All maps distort and filter information. This is what makes them useful but it also limits their use to the appropriate purpose.

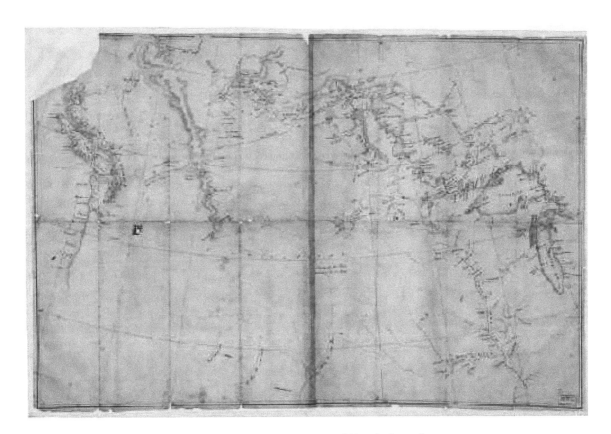

Figure 5 Lewis & Clark's Map of North America

The Origins of Work Mapping

The mapping of work processes began with the early Industrial Engineers from about 1890 until about 1920. During this period, Frederick Taylor developed standardized work and time study. Taylor believed that there was "one best way" to perform any task and that it was management's job to find that way.

F. W. Taylor

Frank Gilbreth was originally one of Taylor's associates and later a guru in his own right. Gilbreth was the originator of the first Process Mapping system originally known as "Process Charting." Gilbreth viewed all work as a process and developed the symbols and conventions that have been most widely used ever since.

In the 1930's and 1940s, Ralph M. Barnes codified the principles and methods of time study and Motion Economy. During that same period, Allan H. Mogensen incorporated most of this early work into a system he called "Work Simplification." Work Simplification emphasized the use of Gilbreth's charting technique and popularized Gilbreth's method.

Frank Gilbreth

During the 1950s and 1960s, Shigeo Shingo used these techniques at Toyota. They were incorporated into the Toyota Production System. The Toyota Production System (TPS) began to migrate to the West about 1980 and became known as "Lean Manufacturing" after James P. Womack and Daniel T. Jones wrote their book *The Machine That Changed The World.*

Shigeo Shingo

In recent years, Mike Rother and John Shook developed and popularized Value Stream Mapping (VSM) with their book, *"Learning To See."* Their approach is oriented specifically to the Toyota Production System (TPS) with individual symbols for many Toyota elements such as kanban stockpoints and workcells. It is unclear whether Toyota invented or even used VSM.

Value and Waste

The elimination of waste is the goal of both Process and Value Stream mapping. Waste is often not apparent. For example, people frequently confuse activity with value-added work. Support functions such as scheduling and inventory control seem necessary and therefore not wasteful.

Definition of waste
Useless consumption or expenditure; use without adequate return. The project was a waste of material, money, time, and energy.
-Random House Dictionary

However, neither scheduling nor inventory control converts raw materials into the customer's product. Both are invisible to the customer and therefore waste.

Viewing waste and value from the customer's perspective is the key to identifying waste. Value-Added (VA) and Non-Value Added (NVA) are also terms used to distinguish waste from useful effort. Here are three tests for waste:

- Does the event or action physically transform the product in some way? If so, it probably adds value.

- If the customer observed the event, would he balk at paying its cost? If so, the event probably does *not* add value.

- If the event were eliminated, would the customer know the difference? If not, the event is probably *non-value added*.

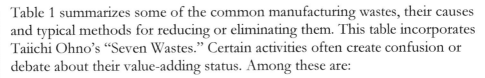

Table 1 summarizes some of the common manufacturing wastes, their causes and typical methods for reducing or eliminating them. This table incorporates Taiichi Ohno's "Seven Wastes." Certain activities often create confusion or debate about their value-adding status. Among these are:

Inspection—This refers to an examination of the product to determine if previous work is correct. It does not refer to inspections of the process as in process control. You should normally consider Statistical Process Control (SPC) activities as outside the process. They are conducted to ensure that the process is in control. Inspection never adds real value since it would be unnecessary if the process were capable and in control. Customers may perceive inspection as adding value, demand inspection, and pay for it. In such situations, we may consider the inspection as value adding for operational purposes.

Packaging—Packaging is often viewed by manufacturing people as some sort of fluff that is not really manufacturing. As a result, they segregate it to a special area so it can be more easily ignored. When packaging is an important part of the sales approach, as in a supermarket, packaging is definitely not waste. However if packaging only serves to protect the product during transport it is waste.

Transport—Internal transport, within a factory or facility, rarely adds value. It is only necessary because the layout places processes far apart. We can often reduce such wastes with an improved layout or eliminate them through a better selection of process equipment. External transports between facilities *may add value* if the customer can perceive it. For example, customers like to purchase fast food at convenient locations and this adds "value of place."

Administrative and Support Activities—Most of these do not add value since they do not touch the product. Examples are scheduling, Human Resource activities and accounting. While they may be "necessary" for a variety of internal or external reasons, they are still invisible to the customer and therefore waste.

Typical Manufacturing Waste		
Type	**Examples**	**Some Causes**
Overproduction	Making too much Making it too soon Making it too fast	Long setups Variable lead times Unbalanced processes
Inventory*	Product not in a value-added process. Idle inventory	Unbalanced operations Unreliable forecasts Time delays Unreliable suppliers Unreliable equipment Unpredictable defects
Quality	Inspect/reject quality Repairs & rework	Uncontrolled processes Incapable processes Poor maintenance
Idle Equipment*	Equipment not performing a value-added process.	Overcapacity Schedule variability
Idle People	People not working	Schedule variability Fixed task assignments Unbalanced work
Talent	Failure to use worker's full mental and physical talents.	Poor hiring Inadequate training Robber Baron mentality Unmotivated workers
Motion	Unnecessary worker motion	Machines too far apart Mislocated tools Nonstandardized work methods Disorganization
Transport	Moving the product	Process focused layouts Disjointed processes Centralized storage

* **Table 1**. The waste of idle equipment is generally overrated by conventional accounting practices. Likewise, the waste of idle product (inventory) is generally underrated.

Chapter 1 Summary

This chapter introduced Process and Value Stream Mapping and explored the concept of waste. We pointed out that no single map or mapping technique suits every purpose and situation. We also explored waste and how to identify it.

Chapter

2.0 Process Mapping

Process Mapping is one of the oldest and most valuable techniques for streamlining work. It is also subtle and requires experienced facilitators for best results.

2.1 Process Mapping Technique

Process Maps (or Process Charts) trace the ***sequence of events for a single item of a single product.*** They may include additional information such as cycle time, inventory, and equipment information. The most useful charts are quite detailed. This is important because much waste occurs at a micro- level.

Frank Gilbreth's original symbols for process mapping are simple, visual and intuitive. One does not need the Rosetta Stone to decipher process mapping. Even with limited experience, a viewer can discern a great deal about the process a map represents. The simplicity of process maps makes them an ideal technique for Kaizen events where training time is limited.

All work or purposeful activity can be viewed as a process as defined in the box. Although, sometimes the process is none to orderly and the prescribed sequence may be vague. These are opportunities for improvement. Some examples of work processes are:

- **Building a Circuit Board**
- **Visiting the Physician**
- **Obtaining a Passport**
- **Designing a Workcell**

Definition of a process
An orderly, prescribed sequence of events intended to produce a product or outcome.
--Random House Unabridged Dictionary

Identify the Product

Process Maps trace the sequence of events for building a single item of a single product. The chart itself contains no information about where the events occur, what equipment may be used or what workers might be doing. A mapping team may add optional notes for this information.

The fact that process map lines and symbols show only events and sequences means that **we must carefully identify the product** and ask, ***"What is being done to the product."*** This is often the secret to resolving questions about how to chart various things. In manufacturing processes, the product is physical and easily identified. For service and office processes it is easy to confuse activity with the product.

A common criticism of Process Mapping is that it does not represent information products or flows. It is true that many Process Maps do not show information flows, but they can show them and often should. To map information, consider it as a packet such as a work order or a database record. Then, treat it as a component necessary to complete a subsequent event.

Conventions and Symbols

The conventions and symbols of process mapping are so simple and intuitive that groups rarely need formal instruction. An experienced facilitator simply explains the symbols as the map develops.

Line Conventions

Input Lines—Short horizontal lines show where parts, materials, components or information elements enter the process. This determines the upstream boundary, discussed later. Figure 6 (A) illustrates.

Sequence Lines—Vertical lines between symbols, usually short, show the sequence of events as in figure 6 (B).

Merge Lines—horizontal lines from a component show where it physically merges with the main assembly as in figure 6 (C).

Information—Process maps may chart a physical product, information or both. Dashed lines can distinguish information when both are on the same chart

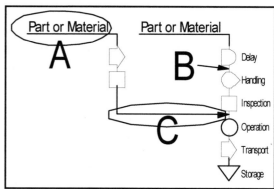

Figure 6 Process Map Line Conventions

Event Symbols

An event refers to something that happens to the product or components. Events fall into six categories as shown in figure 7 and also below.

Operation—These events transform a product or component in some way, usually physically, that brings it closer to the finished product. Sawing, cutting and painting are examples for manufactured products. Interviewing a patient, analyzing a loan application or asking for an order are examples for service products. Operations always add value, but may not do so in the most effective way.

Transport—Transport events move the product a significant distance (say, three paces). Transports only add value when the customer perceives value of place and will pay for it. Transport symbols often appear in combination with the Delay symbols that indicate a queue before and/or after the actual move. Distinguish transport from handling symbols by the distance moved.

Handle—Use the handling symbol for various types of sorting, rearranging, re-packaging or for short moves less than three paces.

Inspect—This refers to an examination of the product to determine if previous work is correct. It does not refer to inspections of the process as in process control.

Delay—Situations that prevent the next process event are Delays. A queue prior to transport is a common delay. Batch operations also create delays since some items in the batch must wait while the others are processed. You should also consider casual work-in-process storage a delay.

Decide—Decision symbols split a process into different sequences depending on some criteria. Use them primarily for information processes.

Store—The storage symbol shows physical products in a warehouse or other official storage location. When items are casually set down waiting for a machine or transport and have no records showing the location, use the delay symbol rather than storage. Information in a physical file or on a computer hard disk is also a storage event.

OTHIDDS—Is a convenient mnemonic for remembering these symbols and figure 7 summarizes the symbols and their definitions.

Operation
Transport
Handle
Inspect
Delay
Decision
Store

Process Map Symbols			
Sym	Name	Action	Examples
○	Operation	Adds Value	Saw, Cut, Paint, Solder, Package
▷	Transport	Moves Some Distance	Convey, Fork Truck, OTR Truck
○	Handle	Transfer or Sort	Re-Package, Transfer To Conveyer
□	Inspect	Check For Defects	Visual Inspect, Dimension Inspect
D	Delay	Temporary Delay/ Hold	WIP Hold, Queue
◇	Decision	Decide Among Several Options	Usually Used For Information
▽	Operation	Formal Warehousing	Warehouse, Track Storage Location

Figure 7

Process Map Example

The example of figure 8 shows the various symbols and lines as they appear on a basic process map. The final product is a package of material for custom sign shops. They use this material for lettering and graphics for a variety of signs and signboards.

The raw material is colored vinyl sheet with adhesive and a backing layer of siliconized paper. The backing paper is perforated so that it feeds accurately into a machine that cuts letters and graphics. The process map of figure 8 shows that the material arrives in large rolls. A slitting machine cuts the material, perforates it and winds it onto smaller rolls. An operator then packages it in a box with a plastic squeegee.

Special Topics

Process Map Boundaries

Boundaries represent the starting point for a particular map and the ending point. The boundaries in figure 8 are the physical boundaries of the facility. The process map starts with materials arriving from the supplier and completes with shipment to customers. An inspection occurs after arrival. In this inspection, the Quality Assurance people remove a small sample, called the retain, test the sample and store it for future reference. The material is stored, moved and processed. Note the small number of value-adding events.

Process maps are most useful at a micro or macro level. Micro level charts show small steps such as "Assemble Cover" and "Adjust Tension." Their boundaries are usually the physical boundaries of a workcell or department.

Process Map Example

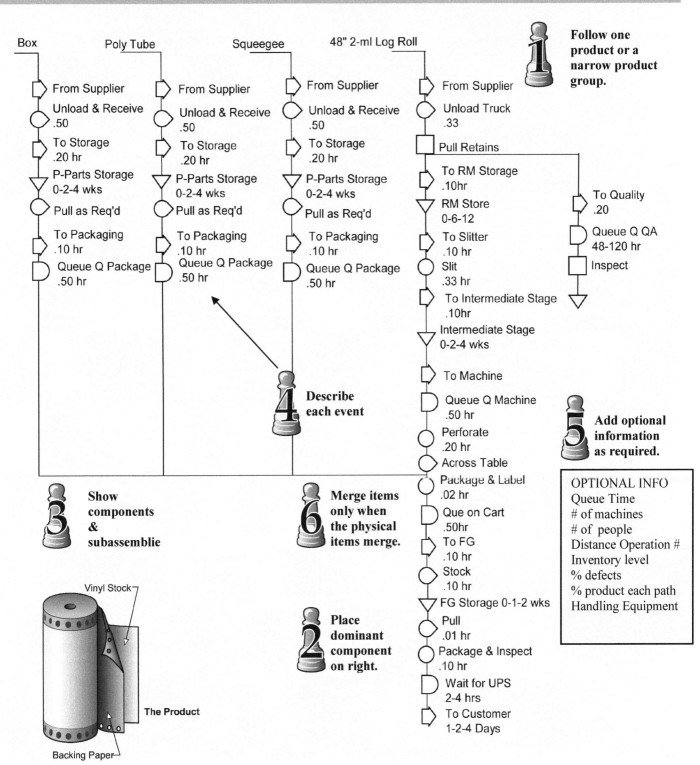

Box	Poly Tube	Squeegee	48" 2-ml Log Roll

Follow one product or a narrow product group.

From Supplier

Unload & Receive .50

To Storage .20 hr

P-Parts Storage 0-2-4 wks

Pull as Req'd

To Packaging .10 hr

Queue Q Package .50 hr

From Supplier

Unload & Receive .50

To Storage .20 hr

P-Parts Storage 0-2-4 wks

Pull as Req'd

To Packaging .10 hr

Queue Q Package .50 hr

From Supplier

Unload & Receive .50

To Storage .20 hr

P-Parts Storage 0-2-4 wks

Pull as Req'd

To Packaging .10 hr

Queue Q Package .50 hr

From Supplier

Unload Truck .33

Pull Retains

To RM Storage .10hr

RM Store 0-6-12

To Slitter .10 hr

Slit .33 hr

To Intermediate Stage .10hr

Intermediate Stage 0-2-4 wks

To Machine

Queue Q Machine .50 hr

Perforate .20 hr

Across Table

Package & Label .02 hr

Que on Cart .50hr

To FG .10 hr

Stock .10 hr

FG Storage 0-1-2 wks

Pull .01 hr

Package & Inspect .10 hr

Wait for UPS 2-4 hrs

To Customer 1-2-4 Days

To Quality .20

Queue Q QA 48-120 hr

Inspect

Describe each event

Show components & subassemblie

Merge items only when the physical items merge.

Add optional information as required.

OPTIONAL INFO
Queue Time
# of machines
# of people
Distance Operation #
Inventory level
% defects
% product each path
Handling Equipment

Place dominant component on right.

Vinyl Stock

The Product

Backing Paper

Figure 8

A road map of Missouri also shows parts of Iowa, Kansas, Illinois and Arkansas. Apply this idea to your process map also. Start a bit upstream from the perceived area of interest and move downstream a bit beyond your area of interest.

For example, if you are concerned with the entire factory, start at the supplier's dock or inbound truck. Include the customer or outbound truck. If the project is a workcell, start with the upstream work center or area. In this way, you capture moves in and out. When in doubt, set the boundaries wide. Events upstream or downstream of the original area of interest may have more impact than initially perceived.

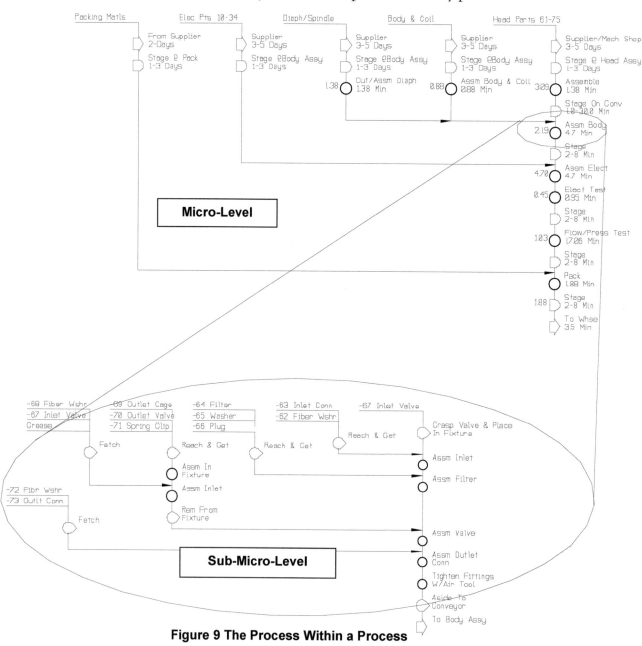

Figure 9 The Process Within a Process

Detail Level

Process maps can depict many levels of detail. Like a Mandelbrot set, every event can expand to reveal more and more detail, as shown in figure 9. Determining an appropriate level for the map is vital. With too much detail, the map becomes too large to see or print; too little and important elements are lost.

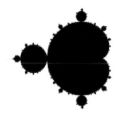

In this example the operation called "Head Assembly" at the workcell level is expanded into more detail at the workstation level.

Macro-level maps show the process on a larger scale and often have boundaries corresponding to the boundaries of the factory. Macro-level maps consolidate small process events into a single larger event such as "Assemble Product." In theory, process mapping could be extended to nano-maps that show micro-motions. Or, It could extend to global value-chain processes. But, usually, other tools are more suitable for these situations.

Most beginners make their first charts with too little detail and often overlook non-value added events. Determining the best level and following it consistently is something of an art that develops with practice. The best level depends on your purpose. Here are some guidelines for various situations that might use a process map:

Macro-Level—This level is most useful for plant layout, Workflow & Group Technology. The objectives here are to simplify movement between departments or develop part families. Operation events normally correspond to operations in the process specification or routings. Often, each operation is in a separate department. When charting at this level, be sure to include all moves, set downs and delays between departments as well as any moves from a departmental staging area to the process equipment.

Micro-Level—is most useful for workcell design. This may require a very detailed breakdown of the events. Once the product families and cells are selected, only those events within the cell or immediately subsequent and prior, need be depicted.

Sub-Micro Level—Sub-Micro process maps are not common but they can be helpful for the detailed design of workstations. At this level, events are quite detailed. In many situations a process map is not the best way to analyze workstations and other tools are available.

Depicting Setups & Batch Processes

The depiction of batch processes often confuses a novice group. The key to untangling this (and similar) conundrum is to recall that the chart depicts *what happens to a particular item of product*, not the machine, the batch or the operator.

From the product's viewpoint, it must wait while a machine is setup and must wait again for other items in the batch to precede it. After processing, it must wait again for the remainder of the batch. Thus, the product sees a delay for setup, a batch delay, the process and finally, another batch delay. Figure 10 illustrates this series of delays. In practice, the setup delay and batch delay are often combined. What happens to the machine and the operator during setup is a separate process with a separate map.

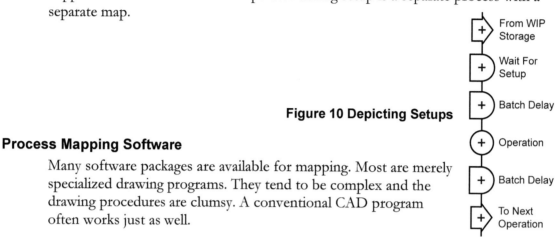

Figure 10 Depicting Setups

Process Mapping Software

Many software packages are available for mapping. Most are merely specialized drawing programs. They tend to be complex and the drawing procedures are clumsy. A conventional CAD program often works just as well.

In most instances, teams should draw their original process map on large sheets of paper that everyone can see. Later, they can use a CAD program or mapping program to make a presentation-quality map. During the mapping session the entire team needs to see the entire map. At the same time each individual must be able to focus on any detail that sparks a thought.

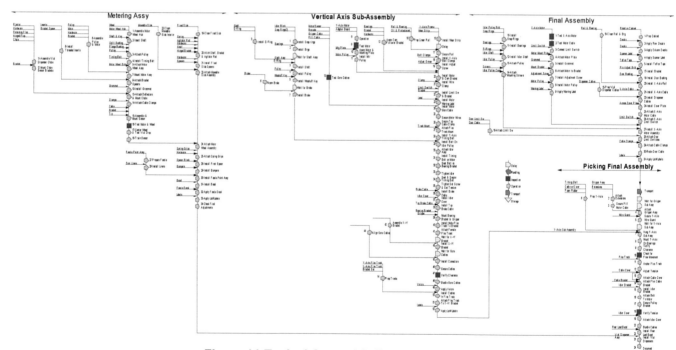

Figure 11 Typical Assembly Process Map

Process maps of complex processes, such as assembly operations, can become quite large. Conventional CAD systems are often the best way to document the map after it is first drawn by the group on a wall. Figure 11 shows an assembly process map.

2.2 Putting Process Mapping to Work

Mapping the Present State

The Present State map shows a process as it currently exists. This is usually the best place to start mapping. Once a mapping team has a thorough understanding of the existing process, they can begin to think about improvements, the Future State.

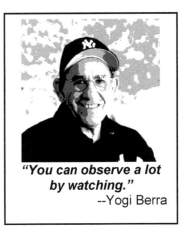

"You can observe a lot by watching."
--Yogi Berra

When mapping the present state, assemble a broad based team from all areas and several levels. It should include workers because they know the details of *what really happens*. It should include engineers and support people because they have a *broad view* of the process and know what is *supposed* to happen.

It is usually good practice for a mapping team to physically walk through the process and observe it first hand.

Chain Curtain Process Example

In this example of present state mapping, a company manufactures several types of closures or gates from ordinary link chain. These closures are common in shopping malls, airports, loading docks and similar locations as illustrated in figure 12. The curtain is woven like a coarse cloth on a sort of loom. To pass one chain through the other, the links on the vertical chain must be spread wide enough to allow the horizontal chains to pass through. After weaving, the previously spread links are closed with a hand tool that resembles an air-powered set of vise grips. Figure 13 shows how the horizontal chain passes through links on the vertical chains. Figure 14 is the present state map for making the curtain itself. The top rod and side members are built and shipped separately.

Figure 12 Chain Curtain Installations

Horizontal and vertical chains start the process the same way. Chain-making machines take cold-drawn wire of 3/16" thickness and cut, bend and weld each link. The machine loops each link inside the previous link prior to welding. It produces a continuous chain that falls into small wooden barrels. As each barrel fills, an operator cuts the chain. A barrel holds several hundred feet of chain.

After several delays at Work-In-Process storage and a move, the barrels arrive in the "Cutting Department." Here operators stretch the chain on tables and cut it to specific lengths for a given curtain. Everything is made to a specific, custom order from this point forward. As operators cut the specific lengths, they drop them into barrels. A barrel may contain chain for several orders.

Figure 13 Link Detail

Handlers move the barrels to WIP storage and then, later, to the "Cleaning Area." An operator dumps each barrel into a tumbling machine similar to a concrete mixer. The operator adds old newspaper, water and starts a 20-minute tumbling cycle. When tumbling is complete, the chain is usually tangled together in a large ball. The operator must untangle this Gordian knot one piece at a time and place pieces in another barrel with many other pieces, thus mixing orders again.

Untangling the chain after tumbling is tedious and somewhat dangerous. An operator raises the ball of tangled chain with a hoist and attempts to pull each piece free. Occasionally the entire ball comes loose from the hoist.

Vertical chains have an additional operation after cleaning that opens every eighth link for weaving. From cleaning or opening, handlers move the barrels to the loading dock. Near the end of each day, a truck from a supplier of plating services picks up the chain, applies a zinc plate and returns it the following morning.

Thus, a dozen or so barrels arrive at the loading dock each morning containing mixed pieces for many orders. Operators remove the chain lengths and sort them into complete sets by order. The chain then moves to weaving.

Weavers hang vertical chains from a large loom and manually thread the horizontal lengths through the previously opened links. When the curtain is complete, they close the open links with an air-powered tool, remove the finished curtain and send it to packaging.

At packaging, operators place the curtains in boxes. Shipping personnel collect these boxes along with the hardware and vertical pieces of the closure. The final closure is assembled onsite.

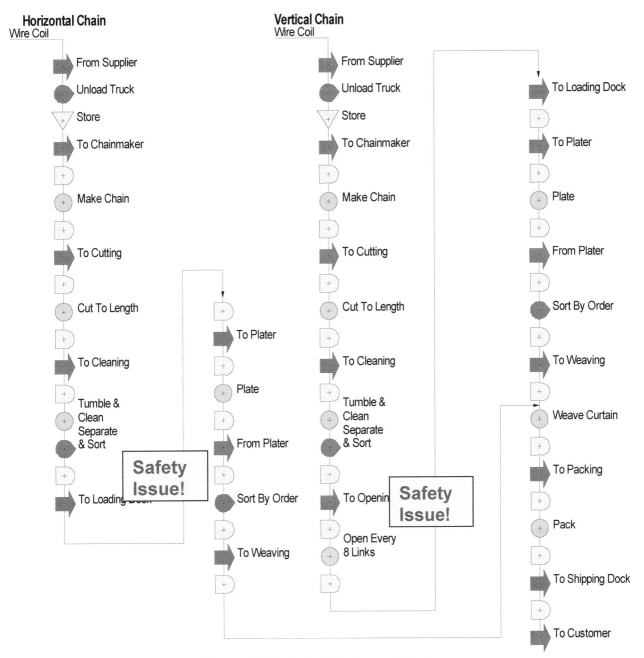

Figure 14 Chain Curtain Present State

Evaluating the Results

Once the Present State Chart is complete, a charting team can measure results in several ways. The simplest is to count the symbols and construct a frequency percent histogram as shown below. This is a crude but effective metric. These histograms show the relative number of each event type and often point to means of reducing non value added events. Elapsed time, labor hours or cost might also be used.

Processes that have not been studied and refined generally show 10%-20% added value. Future state processes may have 20%-40% added value and only half as many wasteful events

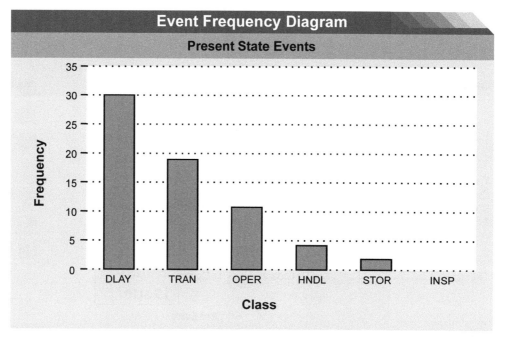

Figure 15

The Ideal State Map

An "Ideal State Map" is useful and easy to construct. An ideal process has no waste so we simply take the "Present State" map and eliminate non-value adding events, as shown in figure 16. Compare figure 16 with the Present State Map of figure 14.

Real processes seldom approach this ideal state but ideal state maps are still quite useful. Their purpose is to remove the entanglements of the current situation in our thinking. It is an example of Edward DeBono's "Lateral Thinking" approach. The key question to ask is: ***"What would be necessary to allow this to happen?"*** For example, the original process of figure 14 shows a delay after chain-making followed by a move and another delay.

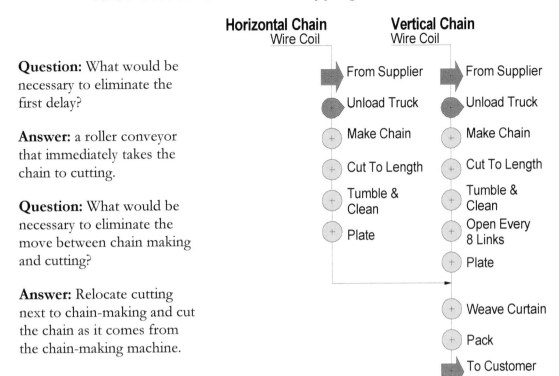

Question: What would be necessary to eliminate the first delay?

Answer: a roller conveyor that immediately takes the chain to cutting.

Question: What would be necessary to eliminate the move between chain making and cutting?

Answer: Relocate cutting next to chain-making and cut the chain as it comes from the chain-making machine.

Figure 16 Chain Curtain Ideal State Map

Designing the Future State

With present and ideal state maps, a team has a deep and common knowledge of the process. Their next task is to identify improvements and illustrate them with a "Future State" map.

A future state map bridges the gulf between the present and ideal states. It incorporates the realities of technical limits, budgets, political realities and time. In many cases, it can remove some of these roadblocks.

Developing a future state map is often surprisingly easy. The primary tools are Brainstorming and the Columbo approach. A facilitator generally combines these informally and directs the group's attention to the most opportune areas. This requires considerable experience and instinct about where those opportunities may lie.

Brainstorming

For a variety of reasons, people often do not bring their full talents to bear on a problem. Brainstorming is a creativity enhancement technique that uses group dynamics to tap into the experience, insight and creativity of all members of the team.

Brainstorming participants should come from a wide range of disciplines. This brings broad experience and increases creativity. The idea is to quickly elicit a flow of ideas and reserve judgment, comment and evaluation for a later time. A good brainstorm session moves quickly with people bringing up new points, possibilities and solutions in rapid succession. Here are some guidelines for brainstorming:

- Appoint a facilitator to note ideas on a flip chart.
- Define the problem clearly and identify any criteria to be met.
- Stay focused on the problem.
- Do not criticize or evaluate during the session.
- Encourage an enthusiastic, uncritical attitude in the group.
- Get everyone to contribute, including the quiet members.
- Let people have fun (Very important for creativity!).
- Encourage people to raise as many ideas as possible, from solidly practical to wildly impractical.
- Welcome creativity.
- Ensure that no train of thought is followed for too long.
- Encourage people to develop other's ideas or use other ideas to create new ones.

The Columbo Approach

In the movies, Detective Columbo solved crimes by scratching his forehead and wondering "why?" hence our nickname for this technique. The method is based upon the Socratic method. Alan Mogensen, Work Simplification pioneer, called it "The Questioning Attitude" and Taiichi Ohno used it extensively.

Table 2 is a formal list of questions to apply on each event. Good facilitators often sense where the critical issues probably lie and direct questions accordingly. This table also shows common strategies that result from the answers.

Persistence is the key with difficult questions. It is often helpful to allow the group several days to think about the issues after the initial round of questioning.

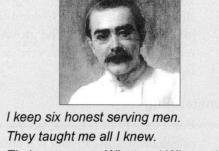

I keep six honest serving men.
They taught me all I knew.
*Their names are **What** and **Why** and **When** and **Where** and **How** and **Who**.*
                              -Rudyard Kipling

Questions for Process Improvement			
	5 W	**Key Questions**	**Strategy**
	What?	What is done?	**Eliminate**
Purpose	**Why?**	What is the purpose? Is the purpose accomplished? Why is it necessary? What if it were eliminated? What would make it unnecessary?	
Place	**Where?**	Where is it performed? What alternate locations are viable? Can the departments be reorganized?	**Combine Rearrange**
Sequence	**When?**	What other sequences would work? Can it be combined with another event? What are the implications of other sequences?	
Person	**Who?**	Who performs the task? Who else could perform it?	
Means	**How?**	What other methods are available? What other process technologies exist? Can smaller-scale processes be used?	**Simplify**

Table 2

Chain Curtain Future State

In developing a future state process for the chain curtain, we used both the Columbo Approach and Brainstorming. From the histogram of figure 15 and direct observation of the process we noted the following:

- **There are many moves and associated delays.**
- **Cleaning seems to leave a black shiny film.**
- **Sorting and cleaning are labor intensive, messy and error-prone.**
- **Untangling after cleaning is somewhat dangerous.**

We initially focused on transports and their associated delays. The most common way to eliminate transport is to place equipment in close proximity. Some of the questions that applied here are:

Why:
> **Why is moving necessary?**
> **What if it were eliminated?**
> **What would make it unnecessary**

Where:
> **Where is it performed?**
> **What alternate locations are viable?**
> **Can the departments be reorganized?**

Who:
> **Who performs the task?**
> **Who else could perform it?**

Several possibilities emerged. If a cutting table were next to the chain-maker, chain might be cut to length as it came from the chain-maker. These operations, however, could not be perfectly coordinated as operators could measure and cut faster than the chain-maker could make the next length. It would be necessary to provide for some minimal work-in-process of uncut chain or the operator would be constantly waiting for the chain-maker

The team developed a large, flat, sloping box, figure 17, to collect chain from the chain-maker. The slope of the bottom was just adequate for chain to slide towards the lower end. Chain could collect in this box for 10 minutes or so. The operator would take the free end of the chain; pull it towards a cutting table and cutoff as required. The operator was then free for several minutes to perform other tasks.

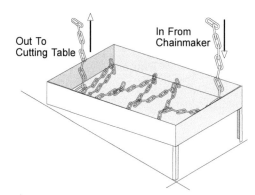

Figure 17 Chain Buffer Container

They rearranged the layout to allow coils of wire to go directly to the chain-making-cutting workcell. This eliminated receiving, a delay and internal transports. They also combined weaving and packing.

The Process Improvement Team then addressed the issue of cleaning. They asked themselves a series of questions about the cleaning operation:

What:

          What are we doing with this operation?

Why:

          What is the purpose?
          Why is cleaning necessary?
          What if it were eliminated?
          What would make it unnecessary?

Where:

          Where is it performed?
          What alternate locations are viable?

Who:

          Who performs the task?
          Who else could perform it?

How:

          What other methods are available?
          What other process technologies exist?

The initial answers to these questions were surprisingly vague. Nobody could remember how or when the cleaning process originated. Nobody knew if the plating operation required clean chain and nobody knew if the operation actually cleaned the chain adequately.

The team devised experiments and discussed the situation with the plating personnel. They discovered that it was unnecessary to clean the chain. Moreover, the tumbling operation that was supposed to clean the chain actually contaminated its surface and made it more difficult to plate. This entire operation and associated sorting was eliminated in one stroke.

Figure 18 Chain Curtain Future State #1

Based on the above investigation, the Process Improvement Team developed the Future State Map of figure 18. The differences between figure 14 and figure 18 are clear from even a quick glance. However, the team did not stop here. They realized that opening of the vertical links could be accomplished on the same table as cutting. This eliminates handling and stretching the chain for the opening operation.

Figure 18 still has several sorting operations after the chain returns from plating. It was decided to eliminate these by placing each order of chain in a separate tote box container. The tote box would contain both the vertical and horizontal chains. This required coordination of the vertical and horizontal cutting and spreading operations. The plating would be done one chain-set at a time and eliminate sorting. In addition, plated chain was delivered directly to the weaving-packing workcell. Figure 19 shows this second Future State.

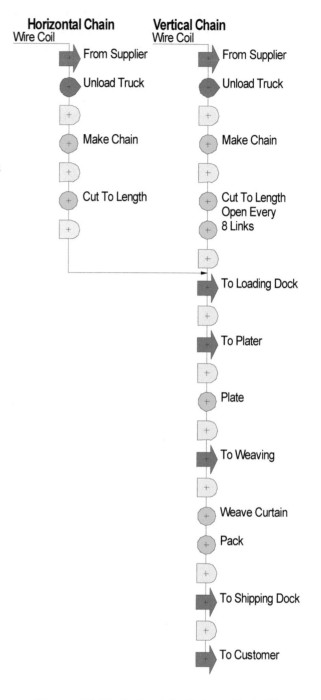

Figure 19 Chain Curtain Future State #2

Figure 20 compares the results. From the Present State to Future States, the value-added percentage of events went from 16% to 27%. The total number of process events fell by 54%.

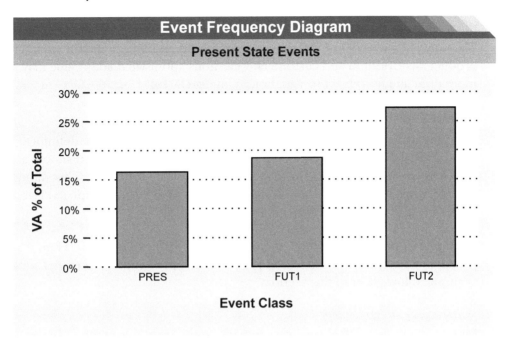

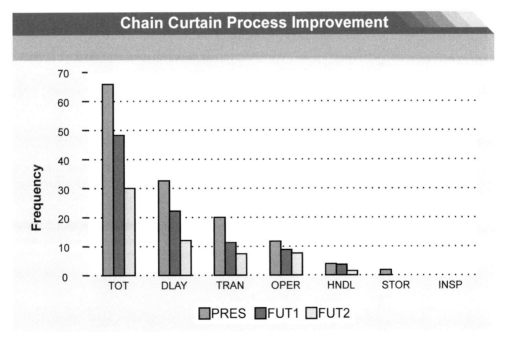

Figure 20

Mapping Information Flows

Information Process Mapping Technique

When information flow is the primary process or relates to a manufacturing process, the techniques for mapping are fundamentally the same as for a physical product. There are, however, some differences in emphasis and interpretation related to product identification and customers. Questions about what adds value may also be more difficult and subject to variation in interpretation.

Product Identification

Since the work product is often ambiguous, it helps to spend time defining it carefully at the beginning of a mapping session. The mapping team should ask: *"What will we have if this process is accomplished properly and completely?"* This should include, where possible, the physical descriptions such as "A completed Purchase Order Form." It should also include quality measures.

Examples of product definition are more helpful than explanations. Here is a product definition for the checkout process in a typical supermarket. An additional example follows later in this section.

Supermarket Checkout
Our product is a satisfied customer moving to the front door with a shopping cart along with proper computer records of the sale and proper payment record (or cash). These three components with quality criteria are defined further in table 3.

Checkout Components and Quality Criteria		
Element	**Description**	**Quality Criteria**
Customer	Customers have completed checkout and have their purchases in hand or in shopping cart.	1. Correct and complete items in cart. 2. Properly bagged. 3. Checkout time less than 0.03 minutes/item. 4. Queue Time less than 5.0 minutes. 5. Customer is satisfied with experience.
Transaction Records	Complete and correct transaction record resides in the database.	1. Each item scanned. 2. Checker properly logged in.
Payment	Correct cash or check payment is in drawer or credit card payment is properly transacted.	1. Cash payment is correct, bills are faced, and correct change in customer's possession. 2. Check payments have a check in the drawer. Identification is confirmed and recorded. 3. Credit card payments are recorded, fraud procedures are complete and credit card is back in customer's possession.

Table 3

The Customer and Value Added

With information processes, the identification of the customer is often problematic. There may be several "customers" within the company or externally. In a medical practice, for example, it is easy enough to see that the patient is a customer and should be satisfied. But patients often do not pay the bills and so the medical insurance companies are also customers. The physician's malpractice insurance company is also a customer in the sense that they must be satisfied that a physician's procedures, skills and training will avoid lawsuits.

Information processes are often for internal use or their purpose is to satisfy requirements that have little relevance to the ultimate paying customer. Many accounting practices and procedures are in place only because of the tax code requirements, for example. The paying customers of the company see no benefit and may be totally unaware of the existence of these internal procedures. From the ultimate customer's view, they are all waste.

While, in a pure sense, the only customers that count are those that pay the bill, many internal processes are dictated by outside considerations, technology considerations or simply tradition. While they may be waste, they can be improved even if complete elimination is possible. As a practical matter, we must often define a product and a customer for these processes and consider the processes as value adding for practical purposes.

Information Flow Example

In the example of figures 21 and 22, we supplement the process map of figure 8 with information events. This situation involved excess inventory, frequent stockouts and late deliveries. The company's goal was to ship orders received before noon on the same day. Orders received after noon on a given day would ship the following day.

Present State Process

From figure 21, the time required for manufacturing to process an order from raw material to finished stock was 372 working hours or about nine weeks since the factory operated on one shift. When a stockout occurred, it required 350 working hours (almost nine weeks) to replenish the supply through manufacturing. However, since the factory maintained significant raw material stock, replenishment could occur in about 84 hours (two weeks) if material were in stock.

Such long factory throughput time precluded the possibility of manufacturing to order while still meeting delivery goals. Since a finished goods inventory was kept of all items, shipment could occur very quickly once the order was delivered to the shipping department. However, stockouts in finished goods occurred frequently in spite of very high finished goods inventory. Occasionally, a stockout occurred in finished goods simultaneously with a stockout of the raw material and this might require the full nine weeks for replenishment.

If a given product is in stock at finished goods, the order processing cycle governs shipment. With this cycle at 7.0 hours, most orders cannot be shipped in time. Reducing the customer order cycle is necessary to meet the delivery goals.

Reducing the manufacturing cycle is desirable since this will lower inventory, reduce stockouts and improve the replenishment time when stockouts do occur. Collateral benefits in productivity and quality are also likely.

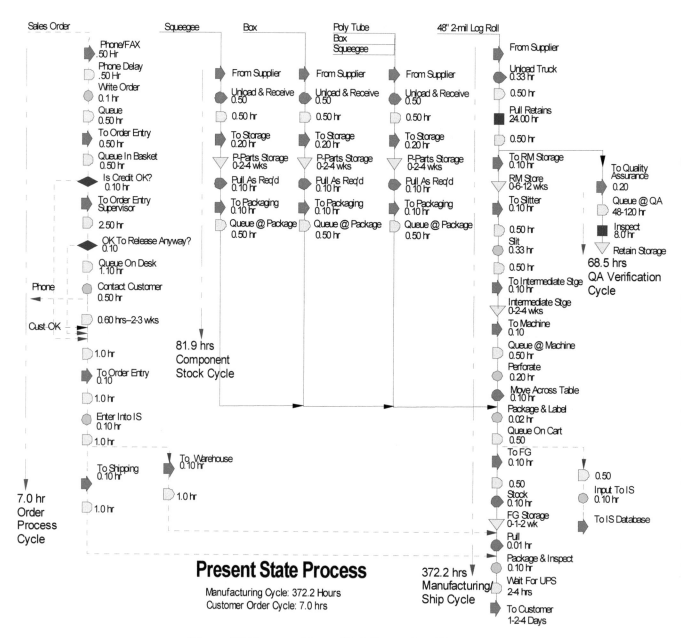

Present State Process

Manufacturing Cycle: 372.2 Hours
Customer Order Cycle: 7.0 hrs

Figure 21 Process Map with Information Flow

Future State Process

Most of the order processing time is spent in queues between order-taking and order entry. Another block of time was spent in the credit-approval loops, particularly if the credit was questioned. Some investigation revealed that the company lost very little money from bad credit. We decided that, for the future state, we could combine the order taking and order entry by having sales representatives enter the data directly. It was also decided to bypass the credit checking entirely except for a few egregious offenders who would be on a manually-kept blacklist. The result was a reduction in the order process cycle by 91% to 0.61 hours.

On the manufacturing side, negotiations with suppliers resulted in delivery of mixed loads of product twice per week. This would be initiated with a kanban signal. Perforating, packaging and labeling were combined in a workcell and the finished goods stock was converted to a kanban stockpoint. The intermediate storage was reduced and converted to kanban. Smaller lot sizes in slitting and perforating assisted the kanban system. The manufacturing cycle was reduced by 81% to 69.9 hours.

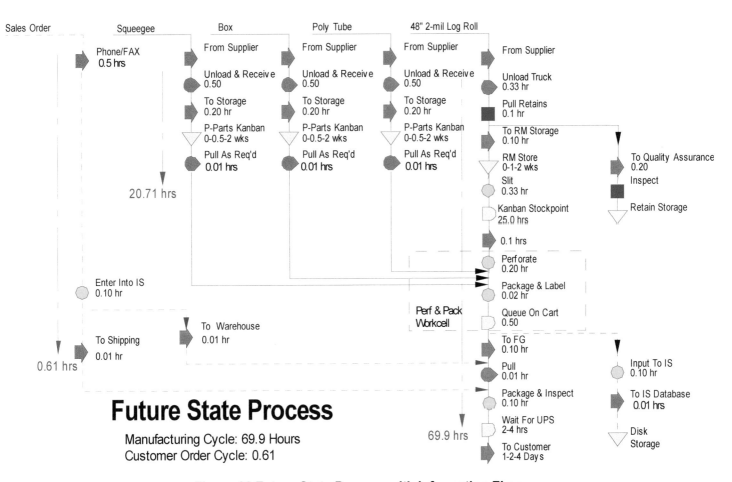

Figure 22 Future State Process with Information Flow

Facilitating Process Mapping Sessions

While mapping is useful for individual thinking, it is most effective in a group setting. In a group, the facilitator is key. Facilitators guide events, question conventional wisdom and keep the discussion on track while the team provides detailed process knowledge.

Facilitators need *not* have experience with the process under study. Indeed, lack of experience is an asset; it forces questions that others take for granted. However, facilitators do need experience with group mapping. Teams do not need training in mapping techniques if the facilitator has experience. Gilbreth's method and symbols are so simple and intuitive that the team learns quickly from the facilitator's example.

Preparation

Before the mapping session, an effective facilitator should:

- **Identify management objectives**
- **Select a preliminary product**
- **Prepare the room**

Objectives

The facilitator should discuss the problems, products and process with management and identify their objectives in terms of cost reduction, throughput time, quality, safety or other parameters. These objectives should be ranked in importance.

Product Selection

In many situations, problems involve a broad class of products that may have different processes or routings. Process Mapping is effective for only a single product or a group of products with high similarity. Try to determine if the solutions for one product will apply to the entire class. If not, separate charts may be required for several sub-classes. Select a product that is fairly typical or representative, not the most complex and not the simplest. A brief walk through the plant will also help. As facilitator, you do not need to know the details of the process at this point. Only a general knowledge of the types of processes and their physical arrangement is necessary.

Room Preparation

Other than provisions for drawing the map, the normal requirements for a meeting room apply. Process maps can become quite large. They should be on a single piece of paper that everyone can see and read. This may require covering one or more entire walls, from floor to a 7-foot height with paper. Computers rarely help in a mapping session. They only display a small part of the map, and the drawing technique is clumsy and they distract from the mapping.

Conducting the Present State Meeting

Introduction

Start with the usual introductions and state the objectives. It is unnecessary to explain the charting techniques or symbols in detail; the team will learn by doing. Tell the group that they will be "charting the sequence of events that affect the product." Explain that they should put themselves in the place of the product and ask, "What is being done to me."

Identify the Product

Discuss product selection with the group and get agreement on a specific product or part number. When items are batched, have the group imagine a particular item somewhere in the middle of the batch. *Have them imagine a very specific item even down to the color and serial number. It helps to have a sample of the product.* **This is important.**

Charting a group or family, rather than a single product, introduces complexity and disagreement. Even a very similar family is likely to have differences in the process. It is much easier to map a single part number and then reconcile differences for other parts.

Determine the Boundaries

First, have the team describe the process in very general terms and obtain their overview. From this, suggest a starting boundary and an ending boundary. Ask the team if they generally agree with the proposed boundaries.

Identify Major Components

Ask some general questions about the materials and components. It is unnecessary to list all components at this time. As each component joins the product, use a horizontal arrow and label it. Later you will start at the beginning for each component and join that part of the chart with this arrow.

Select the Dominant Component

The dominant component is the item with the most events. Facilitators usually select this from their general knowledge. If it should turn out that some other component actually dominates the process, the chart can be rearranged later.

Layout the chart

Figure 23 shows a typical layout. It will likely become messy and cluttered before completion; this is not a problem. After the session, rearrange and transfer the chart to another sheet or a computerized program.

If you use a computer, plot the map on a single large sheet. The map loses visual impact when divided into small 8-1/2"X11" sheets.

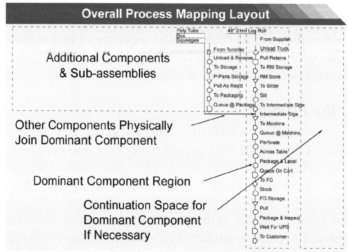

Figure 23

Document the Events

Draw the first symbol, explaining it as you draw. For example: "Let's start where the material crosses the property line. Does it come in a truck? (Yes)." "This arrow represents a Transport event."

Question people closely about events between value-added steps. The team often neglects moves and delays in the beginning. As the chart progresses they will grasp the idea and begin to identify all events.

During the initial session, capture only the events and their brief description. Add work times and other information later. This speeds the session and adds momentum to the team.

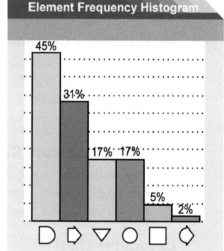

Figure 24

Summing it Up

Have the group count elements and prepare an element frequency histogram as shown in figure 24. Similar histograms based on time or cost may also be useful in certain situations.

Close the Meeting

Ask for comments on the process. Keep the discussion short and postpone any discussion of improvements at this point. Tell the group to think about this process and set a time to re-convene and determine ways to improve it.

Conducting the Future State Meeting
Overview

Brainstorming and the Columbo approach, as described earlier, are the two basic methods for streamlining a process. The facilitator generally combines these informally and directs the group's attention to the most opportune areas. This requires experience and some instinct about where those opportunities may lie.

When the team is stuck, either one of these methods, directed at specific elements, are helpful. Using them formally for every element of the process, however, is time-consuming, frustrating and unnecessary.

Allow several days between the present state mapping and the future state mapping. This gives time for gestation, and improves creativity. Likewise, if the team becomes stuck, a break like this can often help. You may want to have a series of Future State meetings.

Preliminaries

Review—Open the session and have the team quickly review the re-arranged map for correctness. Review the event frequency histogram.

The Ideal State

Either prepare an Ideal State Map in advance or have the team prepare it now.

Discuss Non-Value Added Events

A facilitator normally addresses the non-value added events first. These have usually been ignored for years and they may be surprisingly easy and inexpensive to eliminate. As the discussion proceeds, maintain a list of ideas and opportunity areas. Here are some typical questions to ask:

- "Where are the largest wastes?'
- "How can we eliminate some of these moves and delays?"
- "Can we bring processes together or form a workcell?"

During this NVA discussion, comments will arise about changes in value added events. For example, purchasing new or different equipment. If these ideas help eliminate or reduce NVA activities, consider them at this time. If they simply improve efficiency on an existing value added event, note them and postpone consideration.

Moves and Delays—often are the largest category of NVA elements. Point out that these are related. Moves usually have a delay waiting for the move and a delay after the move before the next event; batching also produces delays.

The usual remedy for moves and delays is to move workstations together, often in a workcell. Sometimes process events can be combined, as when a machinist performs deburr during the next machine cycle.

If batching cannot be eliminated, take note that smaller batches produce shorter delays. If moves cannot be eliminated, smaller more frequent moves produce shorter delays.

Inspections—are also problematic. In some cases they are just plain unnecessary. In others, an inspector does inspections that operators could well do as part of the process. When product must wait for an official inspector, there is, inevitably, a batch and delay.

Handling—these events are infrequent but often easy to eliminate. They usually appear when batches of mixed product are sorted. It is often possible to maintain segregation of the product originally and eliminate the sorting.

Storage—may occur infrequently, but storage and carrying cost is usually high. Moreover, accounting systems often do not capture the true storage cost. Some storages disappear when operations are brought together. In other situations, the amount of storage can be reduced by more frequent delivery or kanban (Chapter 4).

Discuss Value Added Events

Value added events such as turning, casting, soldering and assembly have usually been studied closely. Accounting and management systems focus on them. Moreover, they often require new equipment, extensive investigation and changes involving engineering, quality or other departments. For these reasons, a team usually addresses such changes in a second phase after improving the NVA events.

Identify value added events that have large improvement opportunities. Such events may:

- **Have large wastes or quality problems**
- **Create associated NVA events**
- **Need to be scaled down for workcells**

When it is necessary to examine value added processes, this often arises from a need for multiple, smaller-scale processes for workcells. Quality issues may also force an early examination of the value added events. Finally, some improvements to value added processes can be made quickly and cheaply and these should not be ignored.

Leverage Points

As facilitator, look for leverage points. These are events that, if changed, lead to very large improvements or untangle a complex situation.

Leverage points are often accepted as inevitable and unchangeable. That may be the conventional wisdom, but as facilitator, you have a unique position to question and provoke new thinking.

Ask for additional ideas on the value added events in a formal or informal brainstorming session. Have the group classify them by whether or not they could be implemented quickly.

Once the various potential improvements are identified, lead the group towards consensus on the following questions:

- **"What additional information or decisions do we need?"**
- **"What do we implement right away?"**
- **"What do implement later?"**

Develop an Action Plan

Help the group develop their action plan. This may include additional meetings or even a different implementation team.

Other Tools

Many of the tools such as Ishikawa Diagrams, PERT charts and various graphs can be useful in difficult situations. However, the authors have a bias towards simplicity and we recommend that you introduce these only when necessary and with caution.

Chapter 2 Summary

Process mapping applies to almost any work process and at any level of detail. It is a fundamental approach that highlights waste in any form and does not depend on pre-conceived solutions.

This chapter has discussed process mapping technique, its application and many specific issues in considerable detail. It has also integrated Process Mapping with Process Improvement teams.

Chapter

3

3.0 Value Stream Mapping

3.1 VSM, Introduction & Conventions

Introduction

What is Value Stream Mapping

Value Stream Mapping (VSM) is a visualization tool oriented to the Toyota version of Lean Manufacturing (Toyota Production System). It helps people to understand and streamline work processes and then apply certain specific tools and techniques of the Toyota Production System. This chapter shows how to do it. Chapter 5 addresses the more important issue of what to do with it.

VSM addresses material process sequences and flows as well as information flows that impact this movement. It encourages data acquisition in a systematic manner that often gives additional insights. See figure 25 for a typical value stream map. The various icons and symbols have fairly specific meanings and it requires knowledge of these symbols as well as knowledge of TPS to interpret a Value Stream Map and use it well.

> **What is a Value Stream?**
> *A Value Stream is "the set of all the specific actions required to bring a specific product through the three critical management tasks of any business: ...problem solving, ...information management, ...physical transformation".*
> *--Womack and Jones*

Value Stream Maps reflect a broad view of the process, usually from external supplier to external customer at a given facility. Extended Value Stream Maps take an even broader view and often incorporate tier two and tier three suppliers and distributors.

Like Process Mapping, VSM is most valuable in a group setting. Many of the problems it exposes reach across organizational lines of responsibility and expertise. When a mapping team has representation from all the different functions and specialties, it gains a common understanding of the process and a better position for developing and implementing good solutions.

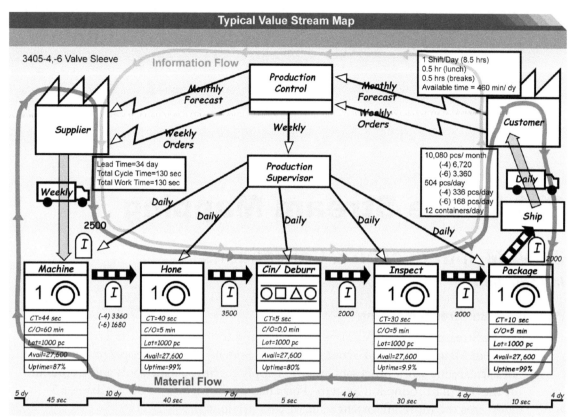

Figure 25

In figure 25 note that information generally flows from right to left (upstream) while material generally flows from left to right (downstream).

History & Background

VSM derives from the automotive industry and was popularized by Womack and Jones in their book "Learning To See." It is not clear whether Toyota invented VSM or even used it in a formal way. This origin in the automotive industry explains some of the limitations of Value Stream Mapping. The technique lends itself well to such high-volume, low variety production. Application in other situations can be problematic.

When to Use Value Stream Maps

As we pointed out in Chapter 1, no mapping technique fits every situation and purpose. Use Value Stream Mapping for high-production, low-variety product mixes with few components and subassemblies and dedicated equipment. In other situations, Process Mapping, often combined with a Group Technology analysis may be a better choice. Table 3 summarizes the important factors and discusses each in more detail.

Application of VSM		
	Applies	**May Not Apply**
Volume	High Volumes	Low Volume may be problematic
Variety	Low Variety	High Variety
Equipment	Dedicated Equipment	Multiple Shared Equipment
Routings	Simple Routings	Complex Routings
Components	Few	Many Parts & Sub-assemblies
Strategy	Toyota Production System	Non-toyota & Variations of Toyota

Table 4

Volume—low volume per se may not preclude the use of VSM. However, low volume often is associated with erratic demand, complex routings and shared equipment as in a job-shop. This is often problematic for VSM.

Variety—the key question with variety is this: "Are the products significantly different for manufacturing purposes and therefore have significantly different processes and routings?" If so, Value Stream Maps will become clumsy and complex. There are situations where there is high variety from the consumer perspective but because of the manufacturing methods, the differences are insignificant for manufacturing. VSM works well for these situations.

Equipment—when only a few products share equipment, VSM can work well. However, if dozens or hundreds of items use that equipment, when these items have different routings, batches and demand patterns, VSM cannot show all the necessary information clearly.

Routings—when all products visit the same equipment or processes in the same sequence, VSM applies well. When there are many routings, different sequences and many demand patterns a more complex Group Technology (GT) analysis is required.

Components—when many parts and subassemblies go into a final product, a VSM map becomes quite large, complex and difficult to interpret. If most items can be grouped in the same process stream, VSM might work well. However with multiple subassemblies or other routing variations, other methods are more appropriate. For example, the assembly operations depicted in figure 11 would be very difficult to represent on a Value Stream Map.

Strategy—VSM is very much oriented to the Toyota version of Lean Manufacturing. While virtually every industry will use at least some Toyota tools and techniques, there may be situations where others do not apply. In such instances, VSM may lead to sub-optimal solutions.

Selecting the First Value Stream Project

For your first VSM project, select a value stream that clearly meets the criteria above and is not too complex; perhaps a product or product group with 3-6 process steps, little or no shared equipment and similar routings. In later sections, we will discuss how to deal with more complex situations.

VSM Conventions

Overview

Value Stream Map symbols and conventions are fairly complex. They represent information flows, material, storage and many specific techniques of Lean such as kanban. A good working knowledge of these symbols and conventions is necessary for proper construction and use of a Value Stream Map.

The symbols are arranged as shown in figure 25. Information symbols represent scheduling, forecasts and similar information flows that affect production. These are generally in the upper middle region as shown. Material and process symbols represent process equipment or departments, storage areas and other features related directly to material; these are also shown in figure 25. The segregation shown is not strictly true but serves as a practical concept.

VSM Process Icons

These icons represent equipment, work groups, departments or suppliers and customers. The time spent in these areas is often value-added.

VSM Process Icons	
Customer/Supplier	This icon represents the Supplier when in the upper left, the usual starting point for material flow. The customer is represented when placed in the upper right, the usual end point for material flow.
Dedicated Process	This icon is a process, operation, machine or department, through which material flows. Typically, to avoid unwieldy mapping of every single processing step, it represents one department with a continuous, internal fixed flow path. In the case of assembly with several connected workstations, even if some WIP inventory accumulates between machines (or stations), the entire line would show as a single box. If there are separate operations, where one is disconnected from the next, inventory between and batch transfers, then use multiple boxes.
Shared Process	This is a process operation, department or workcenter that other value stream families share. Estimate the number of operators required for the Value Stream being mapped, not the number of operators required for processing all products.
Data Box	This icon goes under process boxes. Typical information placed in a Data Box underneath FACTORY icons is the frequency of shipping, material handling information, transfer batch size, demand quantity per period, etc. Typical information in a Data Box: C/T (Cycle Time) - time (in seconds) that elapses between one part coming off the process to the next part coming off, C/O (Changeover Time) - time to switch from producing one product on the process to another. Uptime - percentage time that the machine is available for processing EPE (a measure of production rate/s) - Acronym stands for "Every Part Every ___". Number of product variations Available Capacity Scrap rate Transfer batch size (based on process batch size and material transfer rate).
Workcell	This symbol indicates that multiple processes are integrated in a manufacturing workcell. Such cells usually process a single product or limited family of similar products. Product moves from process step to process step in small batches or single pieces.

Table 5

VSM Material Icons

The icons below represent material in storage or transport. Such activities rarely add value.

VSM Material Icons	
Inventory	These icons show inventory between two processes. While mapping the current state, the amount of inventory can be approximated by a quick count, and that amount is noted beneath the triangle. If there is more than one inventory accumulation, use an icon for each. This icon also represents storage for raw materials and finished goods.
Shipments	This icon represents movement of raw materials from suppliers to the Receiving dock/s of the factory. Or, the movement of finished goods from the Shipping dock/s of the factory to the customers.
Push Arrow	This icon represents the "pushing" of materials from one process to the next process. Push means that a process produces something regardless of the immediate needs of the downstream process. Push generally results from attempting to produce to a centrally determined schedule or work order.
Supermarket	This is an inventory "supermarket" (kanban stockpoint). Like a supermarket, a small inventory is available and one or more downstream customers come to the supermarket to pick out what they need. The upstream workcenter then replenishes stocks as required. When continuous flow is impractical, and the upstream process must operate in batch mode, a supermarket reduces overproduction and limits total inventory. It somewhat decouples processes with different production rates, batch sizes or other differing capabilities.
Material Pull	Supermarkets connect to downstream processes with this "Pull" icon that indicates physical removal.
FIFO Lane (MAX=)	First-In-First-Out inventory. Use this icon when processes are connected with a FIFO system that limits input. An accumulating roller conveyor is an example. Record the maximum possible inventory. A paint booth with an overhead conveyor is another example as in figure 37.
Safety Stock	This icon represents an inventory "hedge" (or safety stock) against problems such as downtime, to protect the system against sudden fluctuations in customer orders or system failures. Notice that the icon is closed on all sides. It is intended as a temporary, not a permanent storage of stock; thus; there should be a clearly stated management policy on when such inventory should be used.
External Shipment	Shipments from suppliers or to customers using external transport. Use appropriate icons for rail or air shipments.

Table 6

VSM Information Icons

VSM Information Icons	
Production Control	This box represents a central production scheduling or control department, person or operation.
Manual Info	A straight, thin arrow shows general flow of information from memos, reports, or conversation. Frequency and other notes may be relevant.
Electronic Info	This wiggle arrow represents electronic flow such as electronic data interchange (EDI), the Internet, E-mail, Intranets, LANs (local area network) or WANs (wide area network). Indicate the frequency of interchange, the type of media used ex. Fax, phone, etc. and the type of data.
Production Kanban	This icon triggers production of a pre-defined number of parts. It signals a supplying process to provide parts to a downstream process.
Withdrawal Kanban	This icon represents a card or device that instructs a material handler to transfer parts from a supermarket to the receiving process. The material handler (or operator) goes to the supermarket and withdraws the necessary items.
Signal Kanban	This icon is used whenever the on-hand inventory levels in the supermarket between two processes drops to a trigger or minimum point. When a Triangle Kanban arrives at a supplying process, it signals a changeover and production of a predetermined batch size of the part noted on the Kanban. It is also referred as "one-per-batch" kanban. The indicator is not necessarily a card; it may be a simple visual signal.
Kanban Post	A location where kanban signals reside for pickup. Often used with two-card systems to exchange withdrawal and production kanban.
Sequenced Pull	This icon represents a pull system that gives instruction to subassembly processes to produce a predetermined type and quantity of product, typically one unit, without using a supermarket.
XOXO Load Leveling	This icon is a tool to batch kanban signals in order to level the production volume and mix over a period of time.
MRP/ERP	Scheduling using MRP/ERP or other centralized systems.
Go See	Gathering of information through visual means.
Verbal Information	This icon represents verbal or personal information flow.

Table 7

VSM Miscellaneous Icons	
Kaizen Bursts	These icons are used to highlight improvement needs and plan kaizen workshops at specific processes that are critical to achieving the Future State Map of the value stream.
Operator	This icon represents an operator. A number next to such an icon represents the number of operators required to process the VSM family at a particular workstation. With shared processes, the actual number of operators at a station may be greater than the number required for the particular value stream being charted.
Other Information — Other	Other useful or potentially useful information.
Time Line	The timeline shows value added times (Cycle Time) and non-value added (wait) times. Use this to calculate Lead Time and Total Cycle Time.

Table 8

VSM Miscellaneous Icons

The icons in tables 4 through 7 are not standardized and thus subject to some variation. When mapping teams cannot find a suitable icon for a given situation, it is perfectly acceptable to invent a new one. Just make sure that everyone involved understands what the new icon represents. Moreover, Value Stream Mapping is a vague technique in many areas. It is often more useful to innovate in a map's construction rather than adhere to some ideal form.

Developing the Present State Map

In this section we will use the example of a Valve Sleeve machining to illustrate the steps for both the Present and Future State maps. This simple sleeve is shown in figure 26.

A completed map often seems complex, intimidating and confusing. It is actually easy to draw by carefully following the steps below:

Figure 26 Valve Sleeve

Sixteen Steps to the Present State Map

 Step 1—Draw customer, supplier and production control icons. Place these as shown in figure 27.

 Step 2—Enter customer requirements per month and per day. The value stream of figure 27 has two similar but distinct parts labeled as "-4" and "-6." If the customer orders in infrequent batches, note the frequency and batch size.

 Step 3—Calculate daily production and container requirements. Production should calculate the number of containers as well (Figure 27).

 Step 4—Draw outbound shipping icon and truck with delivery frequency. Note full, partial or mixed loads. Figure 28 illustrates.

 Step 5—Draw inbound shipping icon, truck and delivery frequency. Note full, partial or mixed loads. Figure 28 illustrates.

 Step 6—Draw boxes for each process in sequence, left to right. See figure 29.

 Step 7—Add data boxes below the process boxes and Timeline for Value-Added and Non-Value Added (Figure 29).

Present State Steps 1,2 & 3

Present State Value Stream Map

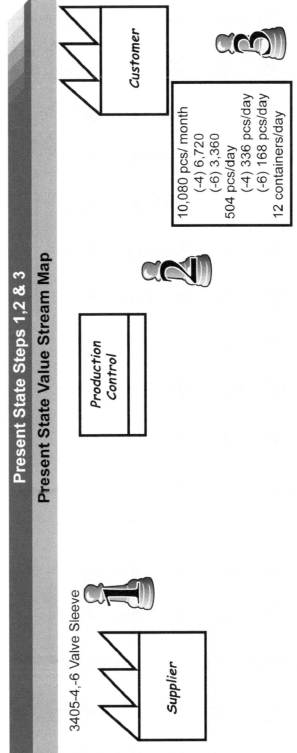

3405-4,-6 Valve Sleeve

Supplier

Production Control

Customer

10,080 pcs/ month
(-4) 6,720
(-6) 3,360
504 pcs/day
(-4) 336 pcs/day
(-6) 168 pcs/day
12 containers/day

Figure 27

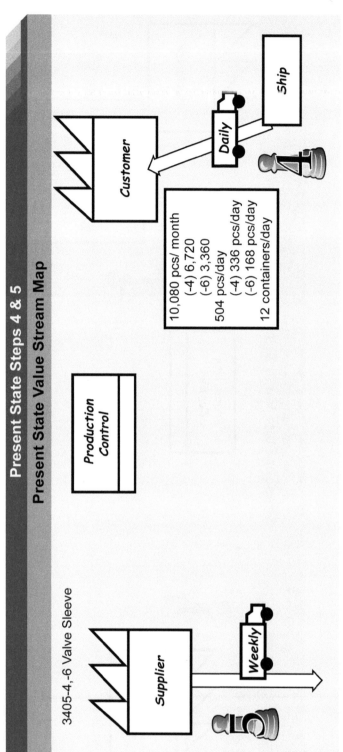

Present State Steps 4 & 5

Present State Value Stream Map

3405-4,-6 Valve Sleeve

Ship

Customer

Daily

10,080 pcs/ month
(-4) 6,720
(-6) 3,360
504 pcs/day
(-4) 336 pcs/day
(-6) 168 pcs/day
12 containers/day

Production Control

Supplier

Weekly

Figure 28

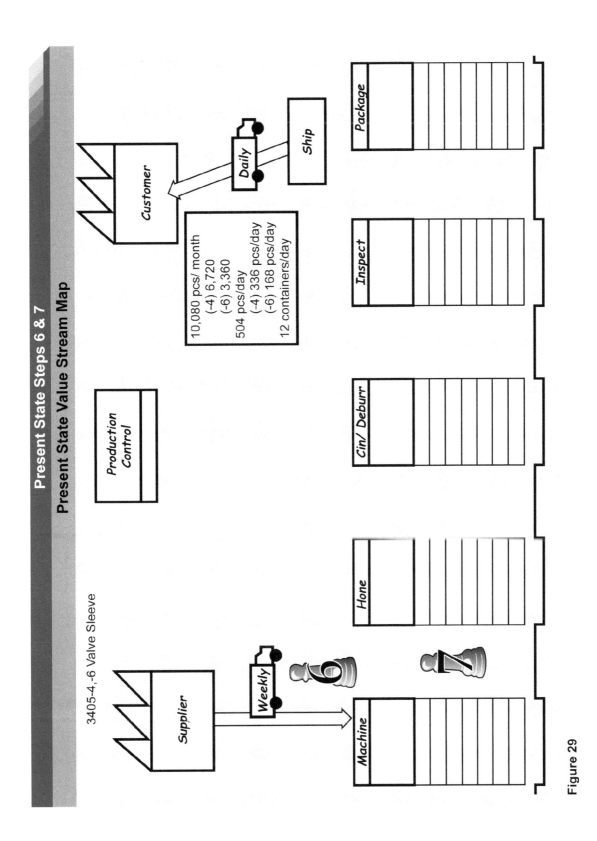

Figure 29

56

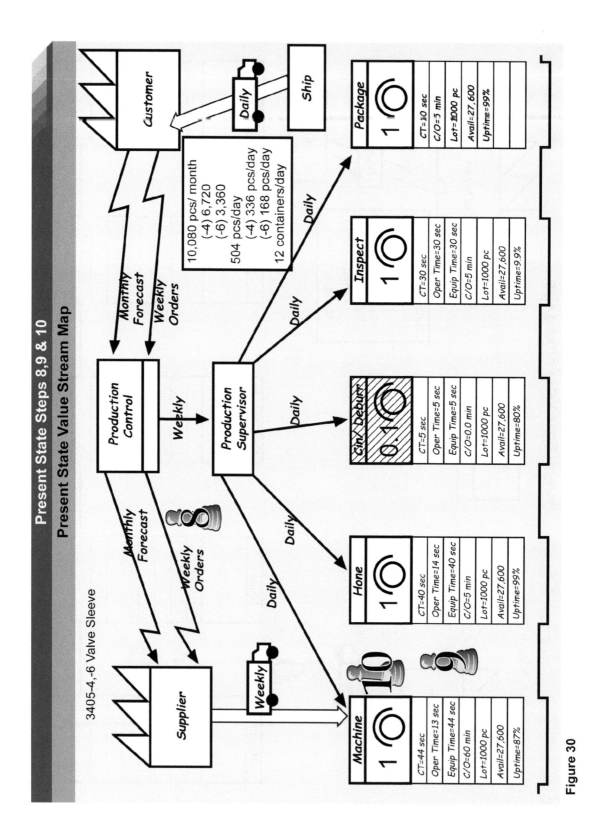

Present State Steps 8,9 & 10

Present State Value Stream Map

3405-4,-6 Valve Sleeve

Figure 30

Step 8—Add communication arrows and note methods and frequencies. This may require considerable investigation. See figure 30.

 Step 9—Obtain process attributes and add to data boxes. It is best to observe all times directly. See figure 30 and the section, "What Goes in a Data Box?"

 Step 10—Add operator symbols and numbers. When the value stream shares a process with other products, use only the number of operators dedicated to the value stream being mapped. This may result in fractional operators (Figure 30).

 Step 11—Add inventory locations and levels in production units (Figure 30).

 Step 12—Add push, pull and FIFO icons. See figure 31and the section, "Push, Pull and FIFO."

 Step 13—Add any other information that may prove useful (Figure 31).

 Step 14—Add working hours. Use the net available hours planned or scheduled for the factory or department at the expected customer demand (Figure 32).

 Step 15—Calculate Lead Times and place on the timeline. For processes, the Lead Time is the process cycle time. For transports it is the time for transport. For inventory point, the section on "Calculating Inventory Times" applies (Figure 32).

 Step 16—Calculate Total Cycle Time and Lead Time. Add the total of VA and NVA times on the timeline at bottom and place this in an information box (Figure 32).

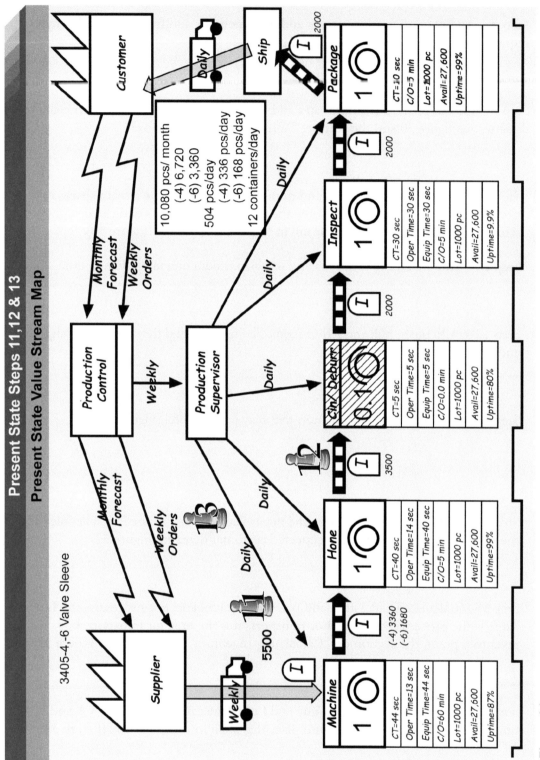

Figure 31

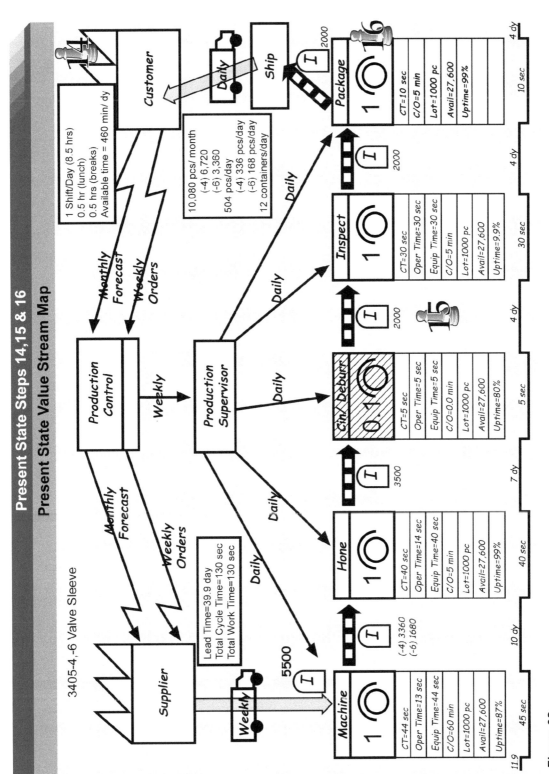

What Goes in a Data Box?

While some authors attempt to define exactly the information in a data box, the fact is that, in practice, the information that is useful varies greatly. In many situations there is simply too much information to fit in a data box of reasonable size and this information must be analyzed separately. You should try to put any information that might be useful in the data boxes provided that the map does not become too confused and cumbersome.

Table 9, below, offers some suggestions on the information that is commonly included in data boxes and often quite useful.

Data Box Suggested Information	
Item	**Description**
Cycle Time (C/T)	The time required to produce a single unit of product and start on the next unit.
Person Time	The time that a person or operator is occupied to produce a single piece.
Equipment Time	The time that equipment or a machine is occupied producing a single piece.
Changeover Time (C/O)	The time from the last piece of one product to the first good piece of a subsequent product.
Availability Time	The total time per day that the workstation is available for production and/or changeover on the product family being mapped.
Uptime %	The average percentage of available time that the workstation can actually operate considering the effects of maintenance and breakdowns.
Scrap Rate	The average percentage of defective product that must be reworked or scrapped.
Other	Any other useful data such as the number of other products the equipment processes.

Table 9

Calculating Work Times

For the Data Blocks, we need estimates of setup, equipment, process and person times; figure 33 illustrates the differences. Traditional time study often assumes that person, process and machine times are the same. This assumption is often invalid. In the example of figure 33, after an initial setup, the person loads the machine. The person is then idle while the machine operates. The person then unloads the machine and inspects the part. The machine is idle during part of this time.

Disparities between person and machine times can represent significant opportunities for productivity increases. Where such disparity is significant, people can load a machine and then move to another process while the machine operates. The longer the process time, the more advantageous this becomes. By placing machines in closer proximity, we reduce the operator's travel time. This allows us to utilize even smaller increments or "bubbles" of time.

Machine Time—This is the time for each cycle when the equipment is busy and unavailable for other work. You may get these times from equipment specifications, stopwatch timing, existing standards or experience.

Setup Time—Determine the time required to tear down, setup and adjust for a new part if more than a single item is run on a particular machine or process. This should be the clock time from the last good part of the first run until the first good part of the next run.

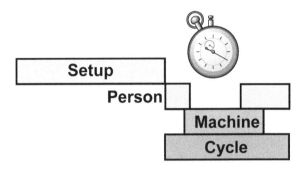

Figure 33 Calculating Work Times

Person Time—We need to know how long a person is occupied during an operation cycle. This can usually be found in the same sources used for machine time.

Cycle (Process) Time—This is the time a part spends in a value adding process. Do not include queuing time. Some processes may require a curing and this is part of the process time.

In situations where a process requires constant attendance, person, equipment and process times may coincide. This may also happen when very short cycles preclude the possibility of a person moving to another operation. You may want to sketch a chart similar to Figure 33 to clarify these times.

Calculating Inventory

To calculate the days (or other time unit) of inventory at each inventory location, we need an estimate of the average inventory in units at that location. It is always best to look and count the inventory physically. However, recognize that at any given moment, the inventory might be much higher or lower than the average. In any case, be skeptical about "official" estimates as well as assertions. Try to get a good overall average.

Once the average inventory is estimated, divide it by the daily production rate for that item to calculate the days on-hand. This calculation is based on Little's Law as illustrated in figure 34.

Little's Law:

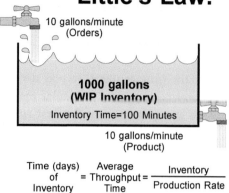

Time (days) of Inventory = Average Throughput Time = $\dfrac{\text{Inventory}}{\text{Production Rate}}$

Figure 34 Calculating Inventory Lead Time with Little's Law

Push, Pull and FIFO

The Push, Pull and FIFO icons show how inventory is handled between process boxes. Here are some guidelines for usage:

Push

Push systems refer to conventional inventory control and scheduling such as MRP. In push systems, a schedule goes out to all of the various processes and each process attempts to work to the schedule. If a particular process experiences trouble, the processes immediately upstream or downstream are usually unaware of that trouble and keep working to the original schedule. Variances between scheduled activity and execution require large inventories between processes. Such systems tend to be complex and often generate large inventory banks. Figure 35 illustrates.

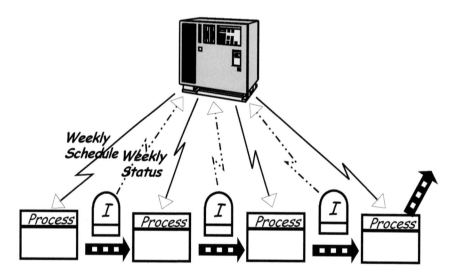

Figure 35 Typical Push Systems

Pull

In pull systems, a very small inventory of every job is held between processes in kanban stockpoints (or Supermarkets). A downstream process simply takes what it needs and the upstream process replaces it. Such Kanban systems work well when a process must produce multiple parts in small batches.

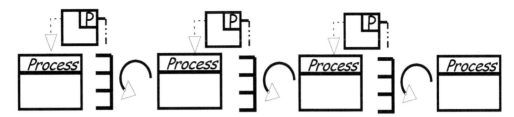

Figure 36 Value Stream Mapping a Pull System

FIFO

In FIFO systems all processes work to the same schedule and process parts in the same sequence. There is a short offset time for each process to allow for processing and transport times. An upstream process simply transfers parts to the downstream process in sequence. The downstream process works on whatever part arrives next. A conveyorized parts washer is an example. These inventory points require little scheduling or control. Whatever goes in comes out in the same sequence and the total inventory is usually limited by the physical configuration; figure 37 is an example.

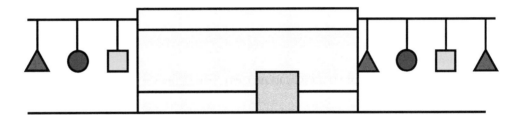

Figure 37 FIFO Examples

Another variation of FIFO is the Broadcast system. In Broadcast, a final assembly schedule is developed and then "Broadcast" to Final Assembly and all upstream operations. Upstream areas such as Sub-Assembly, Fabrication or paint build the appropriate parts in the same sequence as Final Assembly but a few hours or few days ahead of Final Assembly; figure 38 illustrates.

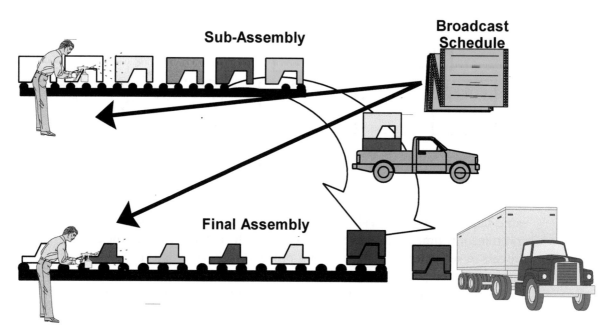

Figure 38 Broadcast Scheduling Illustration

The Future State

Mapping the future state requires knowledge of Lean Manufacturing principles and tools. It also requires an understanding of reasonable expectations for success. There may be several future state maps each depicting a stage on the Lean Manufacturing journey. The future state map is subject to change as work progresses. Some ideas will prove un-workable; other ideas will come to the fore.

Nine Steps to the Future

The following general steps assist in designing the Future State. Keep in mind that, at this point, we are not looking for a final design with every detail worked out. Each of these steps will require considerable detailing before they can be put into practice. Moreover, most acquire a significant body of knowledge to determine these details of design. Here, we are only looking for reasonable possibilities.

Figure 39 shows how to incorporate each step on a Future State map for the Valve Sleeve example.

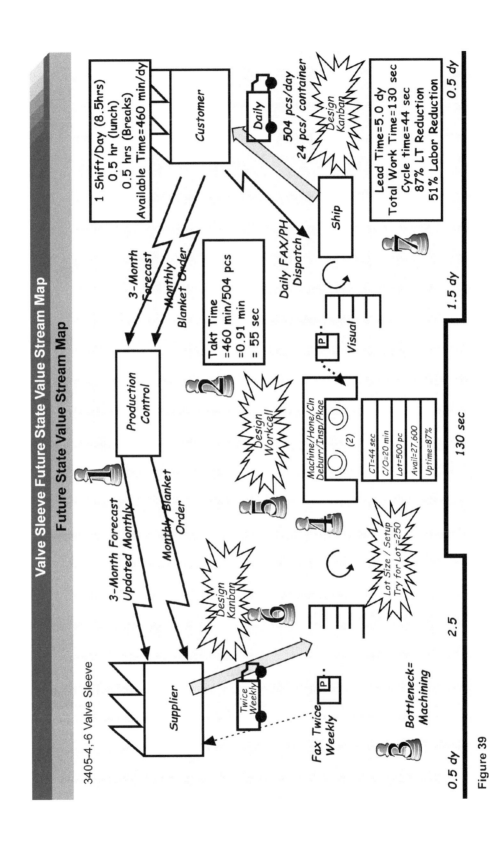

Valve Sleeve Future State Value Stream Map

Future State Value Stream Map

3405-4,-6 Valve Sleeve

1 Shift/Day (8.5hrs)
0.5 hr (lunch)
0.5 hrs (Breaks)
Available Time=460 min/dy

Customer

Daily

504 pcs/day
24 pcs/ container

Design Kanban

Lead Time=5.0 dy
Total Work Time=130 sec
Cycle time=44 sec
87% LT Reduction
51% Labor Reduction

Ship

Daily FAX/PH
Dispatch

3-Month Forecast

Monthly Blanket Order

Production Control

Takt Time
=460 min/504 pcs
=0.91 min
= 55 sec

Visual

Design Workcell

Machine/Hone/Cln
Deburr/Insp/Pkge
(2)

CT=44 sec
C/O=20 min
Lot=500 pc
Avail=27,600
Uptime=87%

3-Month Forecast
Updated Monthly

Monthly Blanket Order

Design Kanban

Lot Size / Setup
Try for Lot=250

Supplier

Twice Weekly

Fax Twice Weekly

Bottleneck=
Machining

0.5 dy   2.5   130 sec   1.5 dy   0.5 dy

Figure 39

Here are the steps. Each is discussed in more detail:

1. **Review the Present State Map**
2. **Calculate Takt Time**
3. **Identify Bottleneck Process**
4. **ID Lot Size & Setup Opportunities**
5. **ID Potential Workcells**
6. **Determine Kanban Locations**
7. **Establish Scheduling Methods**
8. **Calculate Lead & Cycle Times**
9. **Add Kaizen Bursts**

Step 1. Review the Present State Map

At this time, the VSM team should review their Present State Map. This review should answer three questions:

1. **Is the map *essentially* correct?**
2. **Does everyone on the team understand the map in all its detail?**
3. **Where are the major opportunity areas?**

The teams under the facilitator's guidance can only answer the first two questions. We have little advice here other than to question team members closely and discuss these questions thoroughly. If there is disagreement within the team on how to represent some items, you can simply note this disagreement. It is unnecessary to resolve every detail.

Major opportunities may be available where the following conditions exist:

- **Large Inventories**
- **Long Travel Distance or Time**
- **Long Setups and Large Batches**
- **Quality Problems**
- **Low Availability Due to Breakdowns**
- **Delays or Batching in Information Flows**

For the moment, simply note any such opportunities on the Present State Map. You should consider all of these maps as working documents rather than monuments or sacred works. We will come back to them later.

Valve Sleeve Example
In our example of figure 32, the largest inventory accumulations are between machining and honing and also between honing and deburr. However, the entire inventory is fairly high considering we have daily shipments.

Step 2. Calculate Takt Time

Calculate the Takt time based on customer demand. For more information on Takt Time, see the section in Chapter 4. Compare the Takt Time to Process Time for each process box. If any process time is longer than the Takt Time, there is a capacity problem with this process. Discuss the possibilities for resolving the capacity problem. You may use the Brainstorming or Columbo approaches described in Chapter 2. Among the possibilities are:

- **Speeding Up the Process**

- **Additional Equipment or People**

- **Eliminate the Process**

Valve Sleeve Example
For the Valve Body example, Takt Time is 54.8 seconds:

$$\text{Takt Time} = \frac{(460 \text{ minutes/day})(60 \text{ seconds/min})}{(504 \text{ pieces/day})}$$

Takt Time = 54.8 seconds

Figure 40 plots Takt Time for the Valve Sleeve example and the Cycle (Process) times for each process. Since all cycle times are less than the Takt Time, all processes have adequate capacity.

It is usually advantageous to size equipment for a cycle time significantly less than the Takt Time. For expensive machinery, the equipment might be sized for a cycle time that is 80%-90% of Takt Time. Inexpensive equipment such as workbenches or hand tools might have excess capacity and be sized for as little as 10% of the Takt Time.

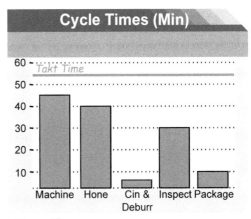

Figure 40

Step 3. Identify Bottleneck Process

The bottleneck is the process with the longest cycle time. It determines total system throughput and is the primary point for scheduling. We want to pay close attention to the bottleneck process.

Valve Sleeve Example

In the Valve Sleeve process Machining is the bottleneck at a 45 second cycle time. The Honing process is somewhat close at 40 seconds. Refer to figure 40.

Step 4. Identify Lot Size & Setup Opportunities

The size of lots or batches should be a function of the setup and storage costs as discussed in Chapter 4. The larger the setup cost, the larger the lot size. Smaller lots are desirable because they make scheduling easier, reduce inventory and enable kanban. However, the lower limit for lot sizing is determined primarily by setup cost. If setup cost and time can be reduced, it allows smaller lots and frees capacity for additional production and for scheduling flexibility.

First, it is important to verify that the Present State lot size is appropriate for the current state setup and storage costs involved. It often happens that lot sizing is done by intuition or tradition and is much larger or smaller than the optimum.

If the existing lot size is reasonable but still amounts to more than a few hours of production, give attention to reducing setup times and thereby lowering the lot size. Setup time reductions of 50%-90% are not uncommon with even simple techniques. Chapter 4 has some additional information. Your team may require considerable experience and knowledge to estimate the size of possible reductions and the resultant optimum lot size.

Valve Sleeve Example

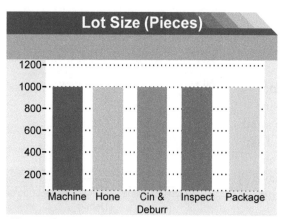

Figure 41

For the Valve Sleeve example, we plotted setup times and lot sizes for each process as figure 41 shows. It is clear that setup on the machining operation dominates the lot sizing consideration. Moreover, all processes are using the same lot size regardless of their setup time. This opens several possibilities:

1) If the machining setup cannot be reduced, we could maintain a high inventory between machining and honing and then operate with much smaller lots in Honing, Cleaning, Inspection and packaging. This might offer significant inventory reductions and improvements in lead-time.

2) The other possibility is to reduce the machining setup time so it is more in line with the setup times for other processes. This would allow us to keep the same lots throughout the process while reducing inventory significantly. The team estimated that a setup time of 20 minutes was attainable. This included the machining operation. Figure 39 shows this new setup time.

Step 5. Identify Potential Workcells

Generally, it is best to combine all processes from start to finish, in a single workcell dedicated to the product or product family being mapped. However, several factors may limit the feasibility of this. Among these limiting factors are:

- A process technology that is only feasible on a large scale that, for economic reasons, requires multiple products. For example, plating processes usually require a large investment in a plating line that cannot be easily scaled down.

- A process cannot be physically relocated into a workcell for environmental, safety or economic reasons. Plating is also an example here.

- A process requires exceptional skill that cannot be easily taught to multiple workers and distributed among several workcells.

It often happens that existing processes are large-scale but other technologies can accomplish the same thing on a smaller scale. For example, painting can be done in a small booth and does not necessarily require a large, conveyorized paint line. Some processes have been isolated for environmental reasons but these environmental factors may be controlled with proper equipment. For example, operations such as grinding that generate dust can be relocated near other areas if they have adequate dust collection. Lastly, special skills are often overrated and can, in fact, be taught to others or built into process.

When discussing these issues, a mapping team should question the objections seriously and explore all options. Many good workcells have been abandoned because people have not thought enough about ways to deal with the roadblocks.

Our purpose here is not to design the workcell but establish its feasibility. Workcells appear simple but are, in fact, complex socio-technical systems that require careful consideration of many factors. There is more detail in Chapter four and the author's book *"Facilities and Workplace Design."*

Valve Sleeve Example

1) For the Valve Sleeve example, it was clear from figure 40 that the processes were not balanced. This is not really a problem within a workcell because there are other ways to balance a cell besides allocating equal amounts of work. See the Appendix for more on this.

2) The shared Deburr/Clean process was discussed and several options developed for scaled down equipment sized only for Valve Sleeve production.

3) Inspection and packaging was combined so the same operator inspected parts and placed them in their shipping container.

The result was a workcell for the two versions of the Valve Sleeve that contained all necessary operations. The future State Value Stream Map of figure 39 reflects this.

Step 6 Determine Kanban, Broadcast & FIFO Locations

In Step 6, identify likely locations for Kanban and FIFO and add the appropriate icons to the Future State Map as in figure 39.

FIFO

FIFO processes all orders in same sequence and batch size through several operations. If this is feasible, then we control the upstream process through kanban or conventional scheduling and the downstream process works on whatever comes out of the upstream process in the same sequence and the same batches. This is extremely simple and requires very little inventory.

Broadcast

Broadcast Systems are a variation of FIFO in which all processes work to the same schedule but with a short offset in time to allow for transport. Production sequences and batches are the same for all processes. Chapter 4 expands on this topic.

Kanban

Kanban systems allow differences in batch size and/or sequence. Use them where process technology dictates different batch sizes or sequences. An example is between a chemical batch mixing operation that produces large batches of product and a packaging operation that puts the same product into various sizes and types of containers on customer demand. See chapter 4.

Any or all of these methods can work within a workcell or between workcells or between workcells and customers or between workcells and functional departments or between workcells and suppliers. For the Value Stream Map, we will not attempt to identify FIFO and Kanban stockpoints (Supermarkets) within a workcell. This will be part of the cell design that comes later.

Valve Sleeve Example

For the Valve Sleeve Example, the new workcell would encompass all processes and it was unnecessary to have any FIFO or Kanban icons between these processes on our Future State map. It was decided to have a kanban stockpoint (supermarket) for raw materials This would allow the supplier to replenish raw materials as necessary on a twice-weekly basis. We estimated the supply as 2.5-3.0 days of material.

The Future State Map does not show the replenishment of packaging materials but this is also a consideration and we would probably establish a similar Kanban Stockpoint here.

Step 7 Establish Overall Scheduling Methods

With the basic processes, handling and inventory methods in place, we now establish the overall scheduling method(s). Some of the internal methods have been already established when we set Kanban and FIFO points.

In general, the more frequently and the more quickly scheduling information is transferred, the better the performance and the lower the inventory.

Valve Sleeve Example
1) The forecast has been extended from a one-month forecast to a three month forecast updated monthly. This allows better capacity planning and helps the schedulers focus on long-term issues.

2) The weekly order from customers has been replaced by a daily dispatch that goes directly to shipping where the shippers withdraw from the kanban stockpoint.

3) Raw material is purchased with a monthly blanket order dispatched by kanban twice weekly. This replaces the weekly orders.

The VSM team considered the possibility of taking daily dispatches and then building to those dispatch orders. This would have eliminated the kanban stockpoint between the workcell and shipping. However, it was decided that this did not allow enough buffer in the event that something went wrong in the cell. If the kanban system works well, this build-to-order system can improve the situation even further and eliminate an additional 1.5 days of lead-time and the corresponding inventory.

Step 8. Calculate Lead & Cycle Times

Add the total lead and cycle times and place this information in a box as shown in figures 30 and 37. The total lead-time comes from adding all values on the timeline. The total cycle time comes from the totals of all process boxes. You may wish to add other information as well.

Compare the (nearly) complete Future State Map with the Present State Map and calculate improvements in lead-time, cycle time, inventory and productivity. Add this in an information box.

Valve Sleeve Example
We expect an 87% reduction in lead-time and a 51% improvement in labor productivity from our Valve Sleeve example. In addition, scheduling and material

handling are greatly simplified. There are likely to be significant space reductions as well.

Step 9 Add Kaizen Bursts

In developing the Future State Map we have made many assumptions about the changes that might be made. In several areas such as the workcell design, kanban system design and setup opportunities, we have ignored the details of how these will be designed and implemented. Kaizen bursts indicate areas where future work is necessary to design and implement these features.

Valve Sleeve Example
For the Valve Sleeve, we will need additional work to design the kanban systems and the workcell. A separate kaizen will reduce setup times and allow our anticipated lot size reduction.

Facilitating a Value Stream Mapping Team

Facilitating a Value Stream Mapping team is not all that different than the facilitation of a Process Mapping team. We discussed much of this facilitation in Chapter 2. There are, however, some specifics that are different as noted in the sections below.

Prerequisite Knowledge

Value Stream Mapping is oriented towards Lean Manufacturing and particularly, the variant from Toyota. For this reason, the participants must have considerable background knowledge in Lean and TPS. Experience in implementation and operations in a Lean environment will also be necessary to gain the full benefit. However, if the facilitator and, perhaps, one or two team members have had actual experience this will suffice. Otherwise, the team will need additional training in lean concepts.

Chapter 4 presents some of the elements, tools and techniques of Lean Manufacturing that are particularly important for VSM. However, you should consider the material of Chapter 4 a bare minimum knowledge. The facilitator, at very least, should have considerably wider and deeper knowledge and actual experience.

One reason for the necessity of all of this experience and knowledge is that transformation to Lean Manufacturing involves a paradigm shift that is unlikely to come from a book—even a well-written book.

Facilitating the Current State Map

1. Start with the usual introductions and state the objectives. Explain the VSM process and show an example. Then describe the various icons. Participants will not remember most of this so you will have to guide them as they draw the actual map.

2. Take the participants through the sixteen steps stopping at each step and allowing them to draw the map. Where data is not immediately available, take a break and assign individuals to acquire that data. When they return with the data, place it on the map and move to the next step. Encourage them to visit the actual processes and locations to see things firsthand.

3. When complete, quickly review the map, note possible problem areas and schedule the next session.

3.2 Putting VSM to Work

Lean Manufacturing Principles, Elements and Techniques

When the team reconvenes, they should review or have training on the various principles, elements and techniques of Lean Manufacturing. The emphasis should be on the topics in Chapter 4. This might require one or two full days if many of the members are unfamiliar with lean.

Facilitating the Future State Map

In facilitating the Future State Map, take the team through the nine steps from this chapter. The primary challenge, as facilitator, is to recognize opportunities that may seem unfeasible to the team and then motivate them to explore those opportunities sufficiently. When the Future State Map is complete, have the team develop an implementation plan.

The Limits of Value Stream Mapping

Value Stream Mapping (VSM) is a visualization tool, oriented to the Toyota version of Lean Manufacturing. As with any tool, it has limits as discussed below.

Fuzzy Definitions
The definition of "value stream" is rather fuzzy. For example:

The map does not even begin to capture "all specific actions."

The definition says "specific product" but the originators apply it to product families with little guidance as to what constitutes a family.

> **What is a Value Stream?**
> *A Value Stream is "the set of all the specific actions required to bring a specific product through the three critical management tasks of any business: ...problem solving, ...information management, ...physical transformation".*
> --Womack and Jones

"Value Stream" conjures a vision of water running through a series of value-adding activities. But many icons do not depict value-adding activities, do not touch the product and do not flow like a stream.

Non-Technical Aspects of Lean
Value Stream Mapping is a technical tool that examines the physical system, processes and interconnections. Equally important for Lean Manufacturing success

is the people side. Factories are complex socio-technical systems that require an integrated approach. For example, Lean Manufacturing requires high teamwork for motivation, coordination and problem solving. It requires an effective mobilization of the collective intelligence of the organization. This is especially important in manufacturing where many managers have a technical bent and limited awareness of the human issues.

There may be quality issues that the company could address through Six Sigma or TQM techniques. Five-S can clean up the plant, improve safety and further raise productivity. Value Stream Mapping addresses none of these directly.

High Variety Situations
VSM was developed and popularized in the automotive industry. Automotive plants are highly focused factories with a narrow family of products for a few customers. VSM works well in these situations. However, in high variety-low volume factories, VSM is cumbersome and unrealistic. Here we must supplement mapping with Group Technology and other tools.

Symbology Affects Thinking
Many VSM symbols correspond to specific Toyota techniques such as "Withdrawal Kanban" or "Workcells." This may lead the user to employ these techniques even when they are inappropriate. In addition, there are other solutions that might be more effective in specific cases. These tend to be ignored. Overcoming the influence of symbology requires broad knowledge, creativity and awareness on the part of users. Rote thinking may lead to the wrong path.

Training
To be effective, a VSM group requires training on symbols and mapping techniques. They also need training on the Lean Manufacturing elements that the symbols represent. This contrasts with Process Mapping, which only requires a trained facilitator.

The Problem of Over-hype
Authors and consultants claim unrealistic benefits and applications for VSM. At the same time, customers and managers tend to look for the "silver bullet." This situation sets up unrealistic expectations and diverts attention from important aspects of complex problems. As with the "miracle garden tools" advertised on television, beware of anything that promises to solve all your problems.

Identifying Value Streams

Automotive plants, where VSM originated, usually have a few basic products with minor variations. They produce those products in high volumes on dedicated equipment. In such situations, the value streams are clear, simple and obvious.

Product-Process Complexity

Unlike Henry Ford, most manufacturers cannot just make "any color as long as it's black." Fragmented markets, competition and sophisticated customers have created dizzying product variety—often with lower volume. Numerous firms have choked on this diversity. In complex situations the application of VSM is problematic because there is simply too much information for a single map. This complexity results from:

- Multiple products with wide variation in purpose, design, and processing.
- Multiple process types with many pieces of shared equipment.
- Overlapped routings where some products use particular equipment that is common to some other products and other products use, perhaps, one of these machines but none of the others.
- Low volume on many products that limits the degree of standardization and limits improvement efforts.
- Mixed volumes—some products have high volume, others low volume.
- Inconsistent routings where several parts that are virtually identical are made on different machines for no apparent reason.

One way to address this is to sort out the separate products into common value streams that, essentially, use the same processes in the same sequence and then apply Value Stream Mapping. This approach works well when the product-process mix is simple or only moderately complex. Where hundreds or thousands of products are made on dozens or hundreds of machines, VSM is probably not the best analysis tool. In both cases, Group Technology can help. Chapter 4 has more information on GT.

Extended Value Stream Maps

The concept and technique of VSM can go beyond the suppliers and customers for a given facility. Figure 42 shows the complete value stream for a simple plastic product such as a cup or trash bag. The natural resource of petroleum goes to a refinery to be made into resin. It then moves to the factory where it is extruded or molded. From the factory it goes to a distributor, a retail store, the consumer and, finally, to the disposal site.

Lean Manufacturing tends to focus on only one small part of this value stream, the factory. Opportunities for cost savings in other parts of the value stream might actually be much greater than within a single factory or facility. However, it is usually necessary to implement Lean within your own facility before attempting to extend lean concepts beyond it. A Lean Supply chain features dependable suppliers that are known to provide on-time delivery and high quality. It features long-term contracts without the constant shuffling of suppliers that characterizes more traditional relationships. It features a very high level of trust and openness between suppliers and sellers and a significant exchange of information about requirements, needs and opportunities.

While extended Value Stream Mapping can identify opportunities for cost savings in the supply chain, changes in the system must be accompanied by radical changes in relationships that encompass legal and attitudinal issues. Such changes are not accomplished quickly or easily in large firms.

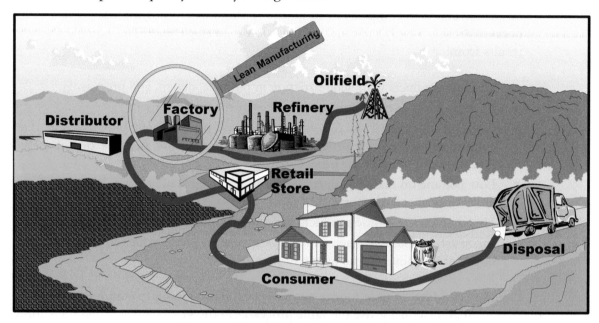

Figure 42 The Extended Value Stream

Opportunities in the Extended Value Stream

Conventional value streams derive from the historical development of our legal system and commerce. Because they have developed from these traditions rather than a rationalized, strategic approach and because they are rooted in a bygone era, they may offer real opportunities for savings and improvements. Here are some of those opportunities:

Transaction Costs
The costs of operating a Purchasing Department and the cost of operating an order processing operation are significant, even when these processes are done efficiently and effectively. Paperwork, bidding, receiving inspection, payments and all of the related activities can add significantly to the cost of materials. When these activities are streamlined or eliminated it benefits buyers, sellers and, ultimately, the consumer.

Poor Communication of Needs
The traditional methods of purchasing and selling are often poor communicators of both the supplier's and buyer's true needs. Many firms have little insight into what their customers really want in terms of quantity, delivery, and function of the product or quality. These systems also tend to be slow and very clumsy. The result is usually high inventories and significant waste.

Large Economical Shipping Quantities
Shipping is often a major driver of purchasing decisions because the costs are clear, distinct and obvious. Since it usually seems less expensive to ship in large quantities,

materials are purchased in quantities much larger than necessary. What is not clear and obvious are the costs of these large-quantity purchases such as storage and obsolescence. Alternatives to large shipments of individual materials and orders rarely get investigated. There are, in fact, many shipping options when orders from various suppliers are combined.

Marketing Costs
The legal environment and business tradition tends to view purchases as one-time events. Buyers ask for bids and often purchase from the lowest bidder that meets other requirements. On the next purchase, a different seller is often selected. The seller must then maintain a high level of marketing and selling activity to ensure a steady flow of business. These marketing costs are expensive and eventually show up in the price structure. In a Lean supply chain, such marketing costs are lower. The result is more profit for the supplier and lower cost for the buyer.

Quantity Discounts
Marketing and other overhead costs tend to be a fixed cost *for each transaction*. A small sale costs just as much as a large sale. This, in turn, leads to discounts and lower prices for larger quantities. Combined with the economics of shipping, it causes buyers to order more than they need and store the remainder for later. All of this introduces considerable variation, inventory and waste into the extended value stream.

Outsourcing

Outsourcing has been the magic buzzword in recent years. Many companies have assumed that outsourcing, based on some magic, will lower their true costs and make their business more efficient. This is often the result of observing the Toyota model where suppliers have played a key role in Toyota's success. However, outsourcing without changing the traditional legal and business model for relations between suppliers and customers actually adds cost to the system and may produce other problems as well. What many managers miss is that ***Toyota has restructured the entire model.***

Characteristics of a Lean Supply Chain

While lean supply chains have many variations, there are certain characteristics that show up frequently. Among these are:

Simplicity
As with other aspects of Lean Manufacturing, simplicity is a central theme. Lean supply chains usually have simple networks with one supplier for each part and suppliers that provide multiple, similar parts. This reduces the number of suppliers and brings stability to the system.

Simplicity also shows up in contract arrangements. Many suppliers for McDonald's and Toyota, for example, have no formal contracts at all. Ordering arrangements and other communications tend to be simple with visual or basic electronic kanban signals.

Short Lead Time

Each facility in the supply chain needs to implement lean within the facility and this shortens lead-time within that facility. Once these facilities are strung together in a lean supply chain, the total lead-time is much shorter than in a conventional supply chain.

TAKT Time

In lean supply chains it is important that all players in the system know the current final sales rate (Takt Time) and adhere to it as closely as possible. This keeps material moving steadily without building inventory at various points.

Very Low Inventories

Simple transports, smooth flows and common knowledge of production requirements combined with the ability to produce to Takt Time result in very low inventories.

Few Transport Links

Because the supply chain is simplified with fewer suppliers, single sources and multiple products from the same supplier, there are likely to be fewer transport links.

Minimal Information Processing

When all members of the chain can quickly respond to changes in demand, there is little need for forecasts. Inventory control systems can be simple and often visual. In addition, much of the usual purchasing and selling process is eliminated or bypassed. The result is much less need for information processing.

Low Cost Implementation

Most elements of a Lean supply chain do not require major investments for implementation. It is primarily a rearrangement of communications and transports combined with a change in attitudes and relationships.

Extended VSM Symbols

The extension of Value Stream Mapping beyond tier 1 suppliers and customers may require additional icons to represent situations that rarely occur inside a factory. Table 9 summarizes the additional icons.

Extended Value Stream Icons	
Cross Dock	Cross-docking resembles warehousing but without the storage. In a cross docking operation incoming and outbound traffic is carefully controlled. Inbound loads with large quantities of particular products are unloaded and distributed to outbound trucks within minutes or hours.
Train Shipment	The train symbol represents rail shipment in our out of a facility.
Warehouse	This symbol represents warehousing and is self-explanatory.
Air Shipment	The airplane icon represents air shipment.
Expedited Transport	In many situations, normal transport by road or rail is supplemented by expedited shipments, often by air. This symbol represents such expedited shipment.
Milk Run	With mlk runs a single truck carries orders for multiple locations. It visits each location, usually on a regular route, picking up or dropping off materials. They are an effective way to provide frequent delivery in small quantities at a reasonable cost.
Orders	This icon represents orders inbound to a facility that are held prior to processing.
Kanban In Batches	Kanban signals between facilities are sometimes held for one or more days before bieng delivered in a batch. This icon represents such kanban signals.
Telephone Communication	Information transferred by telephone.
Control Center	A control center represents a computer or office that directs the flow of orders and coordinates traffic.

Table 10

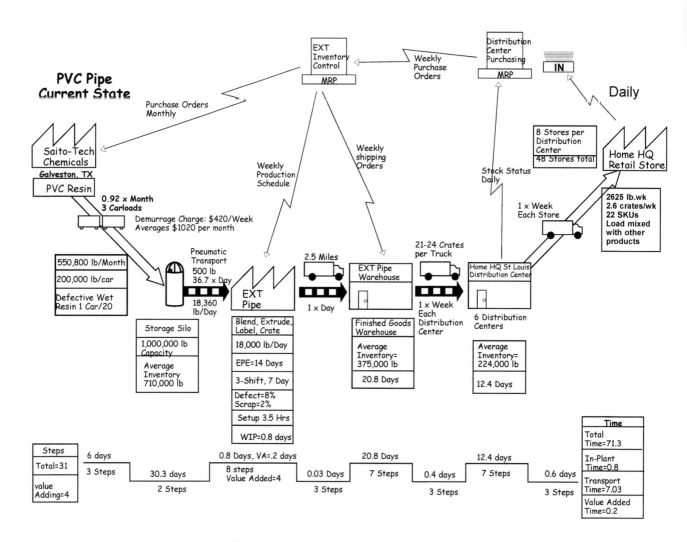

Figure 43 Present State Extended Value Stream Map

In this example (Figure 43) of Extended Value Stream Mapping, a manufacturer of plastic pipe supplies a major home improvement chain. They receive resin from a chemical plant in railroad cars, extrude various sizes and grades of pipe and then ship it to the customer's distribution center. The distribution center breaks crates of pipe and reassembles mixed crates for shipment to their retail stores along with many other items. The total lead-time from resin supplier to retail store is 71.3 days and requires large inventory stocks at several locations.

When mapping and analyzing this process, the mapping team realized that there was enough volume within a Distribution Center's region for direct shipment from the factory. However, the factory would have to supply mixed loads for each store and use a milk-run for weekly shipments to all the stores in a region. The resulting process (Figure 44) bypasses the Distribution Center entirely and actually simplifies operations for the factory. It reduces inventory and cycle time within the factory as well as within the overall system.

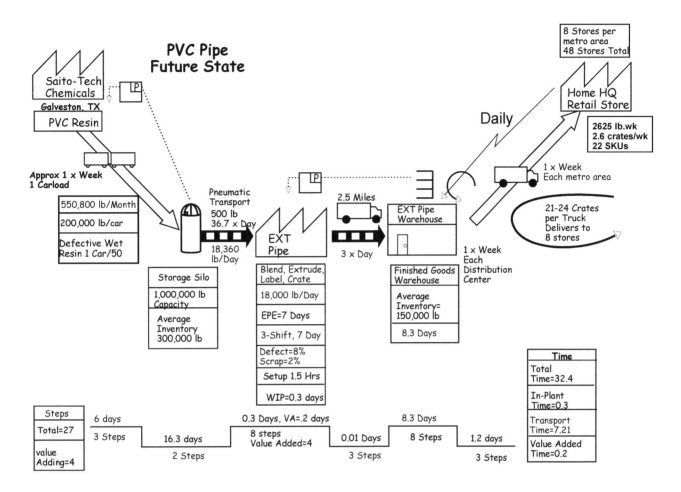

Figure 44 Future State Extended Value Stream Map

The team also changed ordering policy on plastic resin to get more frequent deliveries of smaller loads. This further reduced inventory and eliminated some demurrage charges. The result is a 55% reduction in lead-time and a corresponding reduction in inventory.

Chapter 3 Summary

In this chapter we have explored Value Stream Maps, a powerful tool for Lean Manufacturing. We discussed their application and how they are most useful in situations of high-volume and low variety because of their origins in the automotive industry.

We detailed the way process mapping teams can use sixteen steps to develop a Value Stream Map for their present state process. They then follow a nine-step procedure to explore improvements and generate a future state map.

Finally, this chapter showed how to extend the concept into the larger value stream for even more improvements in manufacturing performance.

Chapter 4 will provide additional information on the particular tools, techniques and elements of Lean Manufacturing that teams will need to understand in order to use VSM effectively. Chapter 5 explains how to use VSM as the starting point for a Manufacturing Strategy.

Chapter

4.0 Lean Elements, Tools and Techniques

4.1 Lean Concepts
VSM and Lean Manufacturing Principles

While a mapping team can develop their present state map with only a limited knowledge of Lean Manufacturing, the Future State map is another matter. We cannot do justice to the topic in this publication, but here are a few of the principles, practices, tools and techniques that the team must be familiar with.

- **The Role of Inventory**
- **Takt Time**
- **Cellular Manufacturing and Workcell Design**
- **Kanban**
- **Setup Reduction (SMED)**
- **Lean Lot Sizing**

In this section, we briefly address these issues. The development of an effective Lean Strategy, let alone implementation of such a strategy, requires far broader and deeper knowledge.

The Role of Inventory

Inventory – Asset or Plague?
Inventory is a recurring theme in Lean Manufacturing. Many authors and lecturers on Lean Manufacturing say it is "evil". Inventory is probably one of the two biggest assets on your company's balance sheet. It is an important determinant of Return On Assets (ROA) and other measures of financial performance. Carrying stock is expensive, usually 20%-40% of the average value per year. It devours capital—capital the business may need for growth. It requires large warehouses and valuable floor space. It increases material handling. Large stocks require massive computer systems for tracking and control.

Yet, inventory can serve many purposes. It allows continuous delivery while manufacturing focuses on long runs. It prevents the vagaries of maintenance and quality from interrupting schedules. It accommodates the variation of incoming orders.

Excessive inventory is not a problem nor is it evil; it is only an effect. Just as obesity and fat are not problems, only symptoms of poor diet and insufficient exercise. The fundamental causes of high inventory, like obesity lie deeper. Among these are inappropriate scheduling, insufficient maintenance, poor layout and a host of others causes.

How much inventory is too much?

We usually measure inventory in "turns." Annual sales divided by average value on hand. This ratio allows comparison of larger and smaller firms. It accounts for changes in annual sales volume and seasonal fluctuation. (While there are many variations of this metric, they matter little as long as they are consistent.)

Firms with outstanding inventory performance excel on other dimensions such as customer service, delivery and productivity. Figure 45 shows the results from one of many studies that support this contention. The study examined four similar firms in several countries. The chart shows the correlation of WIP turns and productivity in units per employee.

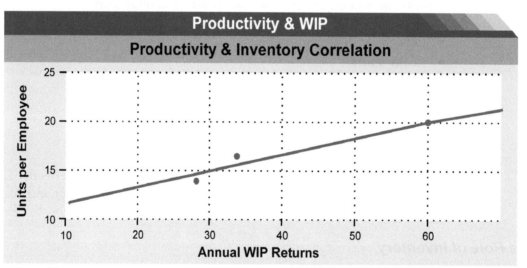

Figure 45

Takt Time

Definition: Takt Time—The desired time between units of production output, synchronized to customer demand. The concept carries backward through a process stream. Ideally, every step synchronizes with the final output. Takt Time is fundamental to Lean Manufacturing.

Calculating Takt Time

The formula for Takt time is:

$$\text{Takt Time} = \frac{\text{Available Daily Production Time (Minutes)}}{\text{Daily Customer Demand (Pieces)}}$$

Figure 46 illustrates the concept for the B-24 aircraft built at Willow Run during World War II.

- The final assembly rate was established at "a bomber an hour" so the Takt time for Final Assembly is 60.0 minutes.
- The aircraft requires one Forward Fuselage sub-assembly and the Takt time for this production area is also 60.0 minutes.
- Four propellers per aircraft generate a Takt time at Propeller Dress of 15.0 minutes.
- Each ship needs two rudders, so Takt time for Rudder Sub-Assembly is 30.0 minutes.

Each rudder requires six ribs. Takt time for Rib Forming is, therefore, 5.0 minutes.

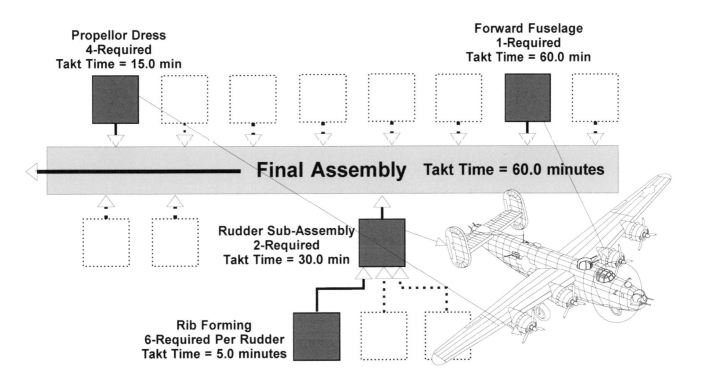

Figure 46 Takt Time at the Willow Run Bomber Plant

Production Miracle at Willow Run

In 1943 Ford Motor Company's Willow Run Bomber Plant was producing "A Bomber An Hour." It was the embodiment of American ingenuity, perseverance and productivity and the concept of Takt Time was an integral part. Here are some of the statistics:

- 488,193 parts

- 30,000 components

- 24 major subassemblies

- Peak production- 25 units per day

- 25,000 initial engineering drawings

- Ten model changes in six years

- Thousands of running changes

- 34,533 employees at peak

- 100% productivity improvement

Benefits of Takt Time

Takt time embodies the concept that production output should be smooth and continuous rather than large, intermittent batches. This output should also mach the average customer demand. The simplicity of the concept belies its extraordinary effects. Among these are:

- **Production Stability-** by limiting overproduction, it stabilizes the system and prevents buildups of inventory and the subsequent stops and starts.
- **Workcell Design-** Takt time helps cell designers. In an ideal workcell, all tasks are balanced, they all require the same time to execute and that time equals the Takt time. If any operation requires more than the Takt time, the cell cannot produce at the necessary rate.
- **Motivation**—Takt time is a powerful motivator. It gives all workers a strong psychological incentive to maintain steady production, every hour of every day.

4.2 Specific Tools & Elements

Cellular Manufacturing and Workcell Design

One of the tasks for developing a Future State map is to identify opportunities for combined process areas into workcells. Cellular Manufacturing and workcells are at the heart of Lean Manufacturing. Their benefits are many and varied. They increase productivity and quality. Cells simplify material flow, management and even accounting systems.

What is a Workcell?

A workcell is a work unit larger than an individual machine or workstation but smaller than the usual department. Typically, it has 3-12 people and 5-15 workstations in a compact arrangement. An ideal cell manufactures a narrow range of highly similar products. Such an ideal cell is self-contained with all necessary equipment and resources. Figure 47 is a typical assembly workcell with four people. They assemble and test a line of small diaphragm pumps.

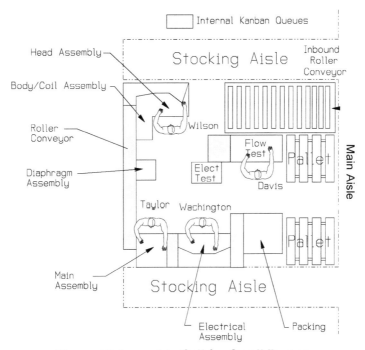

Figure 47 Assembly Cell for Small Pumps

Cellular layouts organize work around a product or a narrow range of similar products. Materials sit in an initial queue when they enter the cell. Once processing begins, they move directly from process to process (or sit in mini-queues). The result is very fast throughput. Communication is easy since every operator is close to the others; this improves quality and coordination. Proximity and a common mission enhance teamwork.

The Benefits of Cells

Simplicity is an underlying theme throughout cellular design. Notice the simplicity of material flow. Scheduling, supervision and many other elements also reflect this underlying simplicity.

Table 10 compares cellular and functional layouts along thirteen key dimensions. It is typical of the improvements possible with this approach. Cells negate many of the tradeoffs of conventional manufacturing approaches.

Benefits of Cellular Manufacturing		
Key Element	**Functional**	**Cellular**
Inter-department Moves	Many	Few
Travel Distance	500' - 4000'	100' - 400'
Route Structure	Variable	Fixed
Queues	12 - 30	3 - 5
Throughput Time	Weeks	Hours
Response Time	Weeks	Hours
Inventory Turns	3 - 10	15 - 60
Supervision	Difficult	Easy
Teamwork	Inhibits	Enhances
Quality Feedback	Days	Minutes
Skill Range	Narrow	Broad
Scheduling	Complex	Simple
Equipment Utilization	85% - 95%	70% - 80%

Table 11

Figure 48 contrasts functional layouts, and cellular operations. The example is from an electronics plant. In the functional configuration, departmental organization is by function (or process). Since each printed circuit board requires all (or most) processes, it travels to every department. In each department, it sits in queue waiting for processing. Ten process steps require ten queues and ten waits. Travel distances are long, communications difficult and coordination is messy.

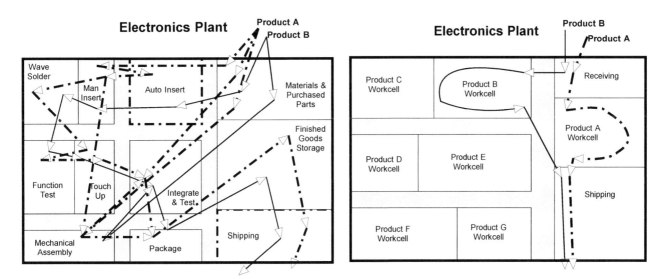

Figure 48 Functional & Cellular Layouts

Designing Successful Workcells

Cellular Manufacturing seems simple. But beneath this deceptive simplicity are sophisticated Socio-Technical Systems. Proper functioning depends on subtle interactions of people and equipment. Each element must fit with the others in a smoothly functioning, self-regulating and self-improving operation.

While cells appear simple, this simplicity is only achieved through a rigorous design process. Table 11 shows the four main steps, the tasks required and issues addressed to design workcells. The intent of Table 11 is to illustrate the rigor required for a successful workcell design. Each step and task requires considerable expertise and knowledge of the available options and when to apply them.

Every cell has fundamental elements of software and hardware. The designer should explicitly specify each element to ensure that it suits its purpose and fits the design. All too often we see workcells where some elements, such as layout, are carefully designed and others come about by happenstance.

Workcell Design Steps, Tasks and Key Issues

Step	Tasks	Key Issues
Select the Products	Forecasts & Product Profiles Chart Processes Production Flow Analysis Code & Classify Identify Preliminary Families	Which products belong together in a workcell? What is the design production rate for the cell? Should we have reserve capacity?
Engineer the Process	Select preliminary processes & equipment Refine the process Estimate setup times Estimate equipment times Estimate person times Estimate process times Calculate equipment requirements Calculate personnel requirements Select preliminary lot size	What process steps do we need? What is the best sequence of steps? What equipment should we employ? How much equipment of each type? How many people do we need? What lot size is appropriate?
Define the Infrastructure	Choose external containers Choose external handling equipment Identify internal production control method Identify internal lot size Identify equipment balance method Identify Quality Assurance methods Assign tasks & identify skill requirements Define supervisory approach Identify compensation method	What methods & equipment for material handling? How do we balance the workload? How do we schedule production? How much Work In Process should we have? How do we motivate people? How do we assure quality?
Design the Layout	Define Space Planning Units Rate Affinities Develop Configuration Diagram Design the Layout	What is the best physical arrangement? How do we handle external constraints? How do we integrate with the overall layout?

Table 12

Kanban

Kanban scheduling systems are among the most simple, effective and inexpensive means for manufacturing production and inventory control. The concept is proven. From Nagoya in Japan to Wichita Falls in Texas; from Windsor in Canada to Geelong in Australia; from microelectronics to heavy steel– they reduce inventory, eliminate stockouts, displace massive computers and slash overhead. They improve both service and quality.

Kanban scheduling systems operate like supermarkets. A small stock of every item sits in a dedicated location with a fixed space allocation. Customers come to the store and visually select items. An electronic signal goes to the supermarket's regional warehouse detailing which items have sold. The warehouse prepares a (usually) daily replenishment of the exact items sold.

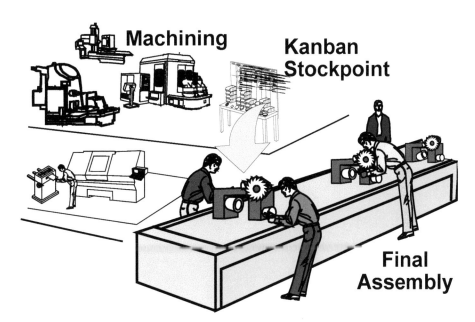

Figure 49 Kanban Between Machining and Final Assembly

In the manufacturing kanban system of figure 49, a machine shop supplies components to final assembly. Assembly is a manual operation with little setup and produces in lot sizes of one, to customer requirements. Machining is more automated and has significant setup costs. Machining produces in batches to amortize the setup and sequence parts to minimize tool changes. A small quantity of each part is maintained at machining. By observing the quantities at the stockpoint, the machinists know what products need to be made and schedule their own work. Figure 48 shows typical kanban stockpoints.

Designing the Kanban System

Preparing for a Kanban scheduling system can be formal with elaborate analyses and simulations. It can also be very informal with fine-tuning done on the production floor. Process Mapping can help understand the underlying process and Value Stream Mapping uses Kanban in many places. We suggest the following steps:

1. **Analyze Product-Volume for Upstream Work Center**
2. **Analyze Downstream Order Patterns**
3. **Identify Kanban Products**
4. **Identify Appropriate Lot Sizes**
5. **Identify Containers**
6. **Identify Signal Mechanism**
7. **Specify Stockpoint(s)**
8. **Specify Initial Kanban Quantities**
9. **Develop Upstream Scheduling Algorithm**
10. **Operate Fine Tune**

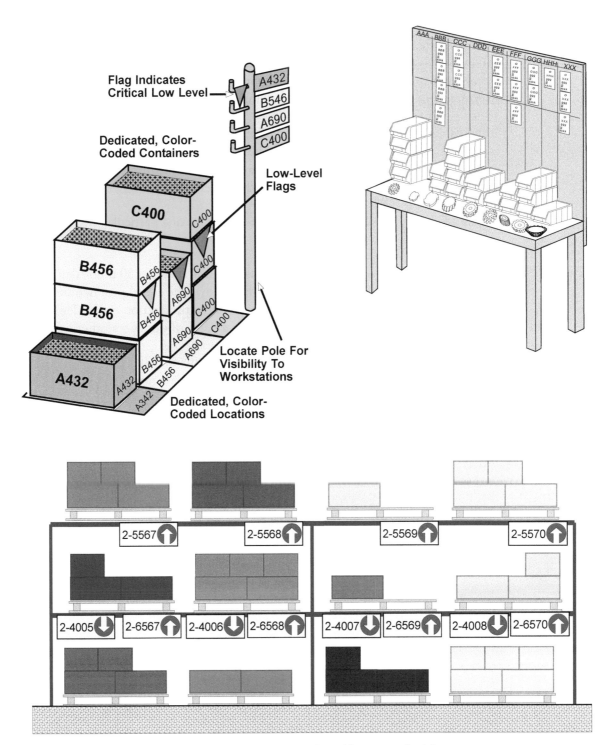

Figure 50 Typical Kanban Stockpoints (Supermarkets)

Lean Lot Sizing

Why Small Lots?

Small lot production (ideally one piece) is an important component of many Lean Manufacturing strategies. Lot size directly affects inventory and scheduling. Other effects are less obvious but equally important. Small lots reduce variability in the system and smooth production. They contribute to better quality in many ways. The most important reason for having small lots is to enable the kanban system.

The Lean Manufacturing literature gives little guidance on lot sizing other than statements such as: "the lot size should be one" or "lot sizing is irrelevant." This section examines the lot-sizing problem in Lean Manufacturing. It offers a rational alternative to slogans, edicts and blind faith in accounting numbers.

Figure 51 shows the effect of large and small lots on one particular workcenter's production.

One line shows daily demand from the customer. It averages 50 units/day and does not vary more than about 30%. The next line shows the actual production if units are made in lots of 80. With this small lot size, required production tracks demand and is reasonably steady. Output is fairly linear with a batch about every other day.

A lot size of 150 units gives is about 3.0 days of demand. This line shows larger; intermittent swings between 150 units and 0 units—quite non-linear. At 500 units there are heavy days of production with about 9-10 days of zero production for this item. This kind of pattern complicates scheduling, precludes the use of kanban and generates large inventories.

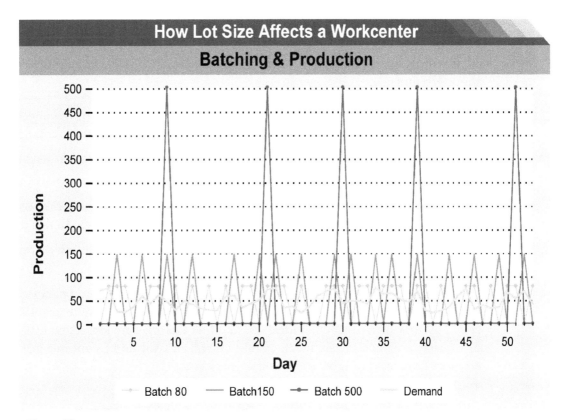

Figure 51

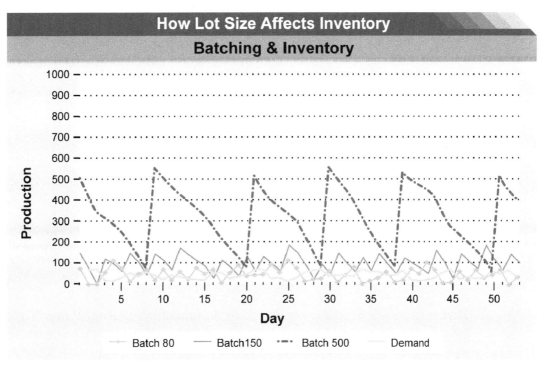

Figure 52

Batching has an even greater effect on inventory. Figure 52 shows the finished goods inventory with batching and a very simple re-order point system. With a batch size of 80, inventory averages about 70 units. With a batch size of 500, average inventory is about 350 units.

Actual inventory would be much larger than shown here because of the uncertainty of fluctuations, the difficulty of correcting a stockout and the need for coping with other contingencies such as breakdowns and defects.

Sensible Use of Economic Lot Sizing

Economic Lot Size (ELS) was first developed about 1913. It balances the costs of inventory against the costs of setup over a range of batch quantities. In this model, the Economic Lot Size (ELS) is where Total Cost is minimum.

Economic Lot Size (ELS) is dead according to some advocates of Lean Manufacturing and Theory of Constraints. They contend that every operation should manufacture what the downstream customer needs immediately in "batches" of one unit. This may be correct in an ideal world. Most factories are less than ideal. Where significant setup costs exist, batch quantity is still an issue and Economic Lot Size provides important insights for rational decisions.

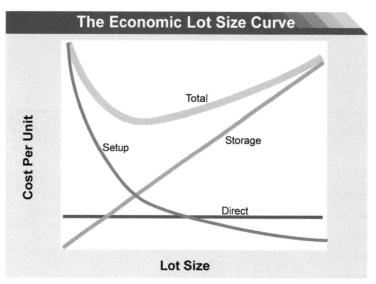

Figure 53

Figure 53 depicts a simple ELS model. This model calculates the total production cost per unit over a range of batches. The batch quantity having the lowest unit cost is the ideal or Economic Lot Size. This Total Cost typically forms a "U" as shown in the figure.

Direct Cost—Is directly proportional to the amount produced. Materials and direct labor is the most common. Accounting systems usually capture these costs accurately and make them readily available. In the figure, direct cost per piece is a horizontal line for all batch quantities.

Setup Cost—Includes the labor and material to ready a machine for production. They may include the processing of work orders or a first-article inspection. We amortize these costs over the entire batch to derive the Setup Cost per piece. This cost curve on the figure is high when batches are small and rapidly decreases with increasing batch quantity.

Carrying Cost—Or Storage cost is the average cost associated with storing an average production unit for the average time it will be in inventory. Carrying Cost per piece (in the simplest case) varies directly with batch quantity. The larger the batch, the more units will be in inventory, on average. These costs are more difficult to calculate and we will not take up that procedure here. Storage costs are significant and often represent 20%-60% of inventory value on an annual basis.

There are problems with using ELS as the only determinate. This is one reason why many lean practitioners ignore it completely. In fact, the theory of ELS is sound. The problems arise in getting accurate costs and in interpreting the results. In spite of the problems, ELS offers insight into the lot-sizing problem and is a valuable first step in rational lot sizing. Here are some of the problems with ELS as a sole determinate:

- Lot size examples in most textbooks show Total Cost curves that are sharp and narrow. Such curves indicate a clear optimum. Yet, most real curves are flat and broad.
- There is a theoretical optimum where (dx/dy)=0.00. But, often, on both sides of this optimum, large changes in lot size bring miniscule changes in cost. This indicates that there is a range of realistic lot sizes rather than a clear optimum.
- The accuracy of the costs used in this analysis is usually questionable. Direct Costs are often accurate and easily obtained. Setup Costs are more variable but a reasonable estimate can usually be made. Storage Costs are often buried in overhead accounts. They must be found and allocated to production units. This makes the Storage Cost component very approximate.
- The flatness of the curve and uncertainty of the input costs suggests that the ELS analysis should be a guide rather than an absolute decision tool.

Lot Size Guidelines

Most manufacturers have never done an ELS analysis. They determine batches by instinct, tradition or guess. Thus, most batches are far too big. Occasionally, they are too small. An initial ELS analysis provides a range of lot sizes. Sometimes it is a very wide range. This raises the question "What other criteria can help select the lot size within the ELS Range?" Some general guidelines follow.

- Bias decisions towards the lowest reasonable lot size. This reduces capital requirements, smoothes production and makes scheduling more flexible. The ELS does not capture intangible costs of larger lots such as quality and scheduling flexibility. In addition, most accounting systems under-estimate carrying costs.

- When a particular machine is a "bottleneck" and needs to operate at maximum capacity, set lot sizes at the upper end of the ELS range. This increases inventory buffers before and after the bottleneck operation but it allows more time for production and less time for setups.

- When a piece of equipment must be staffed and maintained even when idle, and if the equipment is not a bottleneck, set the lot sizes at or below the ELS range. This decreases inventory but does not increase setup cost since operators are idle part of the time.

- Given the fuzziness of the numbers, set lot sizes to a convenient unit such as "1-day of production," "two containers" or some round number.

- If setup cost is reduced, the ELS curve may change drastically. It will become flatter and the minimum will occur at a smaller lot size.

Setup Reduction (SMED)

Setup reduction and fast, predictable setups enable Lean Manufacturing. Setup reduction reduces setup cost, allows small lot production, smoothes flow, and improves kanban. Setup reduction is often surprisingly easy and simple. It is not uncommon to see 50%-90% reductions in setup time.

Setup Reduction (often known as Single Minute Exchange of Die or SMED) seems like a mundane aspect of Lean Manufacturing and is often ignored. However it can be critical because of the systemic (Vicious Circle) effects

When we run large lots of each product, setups on that product are infrequent. Setups take skill, practice and coaching, much like golf. When operators perform setups infrequently they do not learn them well. This leads to the perception that setups are difficult and risky. (You never know how long it will take or whether the product will be right). The perceptions of risk and difficulty encourage large lots and thus fewer setups.

With large lots, a fixed setup cost is amortized over a large number of units. This seems to reduce the unit cost. There are offsetting costs associated with the resulting inventories, but these offsetting costs are usually buried in the overhead. This also encourages large lots or runs.

The consequence is high inventory and complex scheduling. These give rise to a plethora of costs and negative consequences. The black hole of overhead sucks in most of the costs so they are seldom recognized. Other penalties such as erratic deliveries are far removed from the fundamental cause and it is difficult to link cause and effect. Limiting mechanisms do prevent lot sizes from going to infinity but these are often weak.

How to Reduce Setups

Setup reduction should be approached in four phases or stages as illustrated below. Is usually best to repeat the process through several iterations spaced several months apart. The initial phases of setup reduction (SMED) are straightforward and easy; yet often bring the greatest benefits. People are constantly amazed at how much time is wasted through disorganization and general messiness. Figure 54 illustrates the phases of setup reduction as described below.

1. Maintenance, Organization and Housekeeping

It often happens that setup problems are related to poor maintenance such as worn parts, worn tooling, dirt, or damaged threads. Disorganization and poor housekeeping are also contributors to setup problems. These are easy to fix and should be a first step.

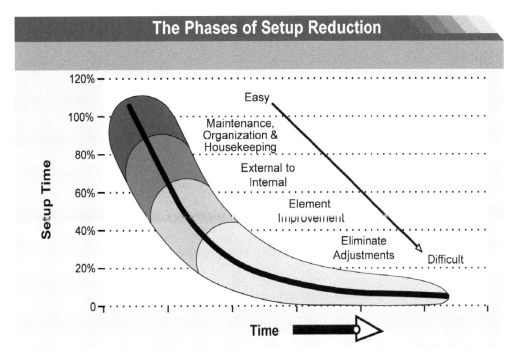

Figure 54

2. Internal Elements to External

Internal elements occur when the machine is down. Examine each internal element and see if it cannot be done externally. For example, the pre-heating of an injection-molding die could be done before it goes into the machine.

3. Improve Elements

Here we examine every element to see how we can eliminate it, simplify it, reduce the time required or improve it in some other way. Improving elements and eliminating adjustments will require more imagination, time and cost. Even here, the improvements are sometimes astonishingly simple and easy.

4. Eliminate Adjustments

Adjustments are often the most time consuming, frustrating and error prone parts of a setup. There are many ways to eliminate them entirely and this is the ultimate goal.

The "Kaizen Event" or "Blitz" is an excellent vehicle for setup reduction. It generates enthusiasm and fast results that make the efforts less mundane.

Group Technology

Group Technology (GT) examines products, parts and assemblies. It then groups similar items to simplify design, manufacturing, purchasing and other business processes. Figures 55 illustrates how an apparently random collection of items has surprising similarity.

 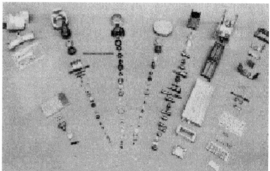

Figure 55 Ungrouped and Grouped Parts

Group Technology uses three fundamental approaches to identify similar products that can have common value streams. These are Intuitive Grouping, Production Flow Analysis and Coding & Classification.

Intuitive Grouping

Intuitive grouping (Figure 56) is the simplest and most common method of creating part families. Experienced engineers and shop people examine the product mix and separate products and parts into processing families represented by value streams.

Intuitive grouping is fast and simple. However, when parts and processes are a complex mix, the method does not give good results. With more than about 100 parts and more than a dozen or so processes, Production Flow Analysis (PFA) or Coding & Classification is indicated.

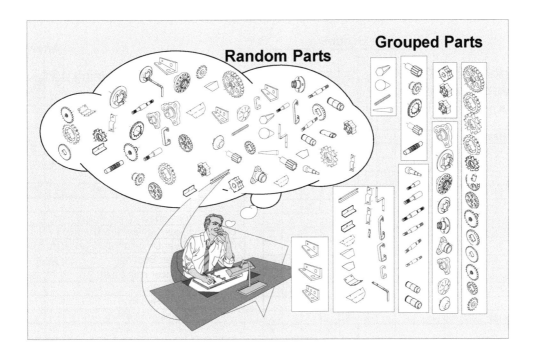

Figure 56 Intuitive Grouping

Production Flow Analysis

Production Flow Analysis (PFA) uses a matrix of part numbers and machine numbers to group families. In the matrices below, columns represent the machines whose numbers and names are at the top. Rows represent parts whose numbers and names are on the left. When a particular part requires a particular machine, the "X" is at the intersection of that row and column.

It is difficult to see order or similarity in the first matrix of figure 57. Rearranging the rows and columns, as in the second matrix, clearly shows families of similar parts and the machines required to build them. These machines form a value stream and a workcell.

This example illustrates the principle but it oversimplifies. In practice, these matrices can become quite large. A matrix with more than a few hundred parts and 20 or so machines becomes unwieldy for manual manipulation.

Analysts encounter inconsistent routings in most PFA analyses. If the product mix is not too complex, they can make intuitive manual adjustments. When the product mix becomes larger than 100 or so items, PFA becomes too cumbersome and a Coding & Classification analysis is indicated.

Before Grouping

Pump Machining Production Flow Analysis		Broach	HMC	Lathe-Chuck	Hob	Lathe-Manual	Hob	Lathe-Bar	Lathe-Vert
61354	Cover Bearing			X					
70852	Gear Driven 8P,56T, RH	X		X	X		X		
52594	Spacer,cplg Shaft							X	
81357-T	Impellor	X		X					
50547-D	Gland, MU, 6"					X			
70935	Gear,Driven,8P,26T,LH	X		X	X		X		
51171	Retainer Bushing							X	
81176	Body Volute		X						X
72298	Elbow, Relief Valve		X						
50763	Spacer, Bearing							X	
71972-8	Adapter, Intake, 8"			X		X			X
62575	Shaft Shift							X	
63160	Seat, Spring							X	
62966	Generator, Tach Pulse			X	X				
71928	Head, Pump					X			X

After Grouping

Pump Machining Production Flow Analysis		Lathe-Manual	Lathe-Vert	HMC	Lathe-Chuck	Broach	Hob	Lathe-Bar
50547-D	Gland, MU, 6"	X						
71928	Head, Pump	X	X					
71972-8	Adapter, Intake, 8"	X	X	X				
81176	Body Volute		X	X				
72298	Elbow, Relief Valve			X				
81357-T	Impellor				X	X		
62966	Generator, Tach Pulse				X		X	
70852	Gear Driven 8P,56T, RH				X	X	X	
70935	Gear,Driven,8P,26T,LH				X	X	X	
61354	Cover Bearing				X			
52594	Spacer,cplg Shaft							X
62575	Shaft Shift							X
63160	Seat, Spring							X
51171	Retainer Bushing							X
50763	Spacer, Bearing							X

(Annotations on the After Grouping matrix: "Turn-Mill Cell" grouping Lathe-Manual/Lathe-Vert/HMC; "Chucking Lathe Cell" grouping Lathe-Chuck/Broach/Hob; "Barfeed Lathe Cell" grouping Lathe-Bar.)

Figure 57 A Simple Production Flow Analysis Matrix

Coding & Classification

With extremely large and complex product mixes, Coding & Classification offers a method to analyze, simplify and rationalize. C&C associates a "Code Number" with every part number. This code number contains information about the product features and processes for making the part. By grouping similar code numbers, the analyst can identify families of highly similar parts that will make good candidates for a workcell. Parts with similar physical characteristics should usually have similar processes. The coding system allows an analyst to standardize process routings and then group the parts into families.

Additional Lean Tools & Techniques

Value Stream Mapping focuses on Workflow, information flows that impact the workflow, and the arrangement of processes on the plant floor. VSM and other methods of analyzing workflow are a good first step towards Lean Manufacturing. However, this is less than half the story. An effective Lean Strategy includes many additional techniques for addressing quality, maintenance and a host of cultural and people-related issues. Among these additional techniques are:

- Total Quality/Six Sigma Teams
- Metrics & Measurements
- Mixed Model Production
- 5S
- Autonomation
- Pokayoke
- Jidoka

- Total Productive Maintenance
- One Piece Flow
- Standard Work
- Visual Management
- In Station Process Quality
- Level Production
- Supplier Development

In a given factory, some of these additional techniques may apply and some may not. A brief summary and glossary is in Appendix. I.

Chapter 4 Summary

This chapter has reviewed some of the tools, techniques and elements of Lean Manufacturing that a mapping team will require. However, there is much more to learn for a successful lean implementation. Readers can find additional information in the Appendix and at the Enna website, www.enna.com.

5.0 Mapping & Strategy

5.1 What is Manufacturing Strategy?

Definition

The word "strategy" derives from "strategos," an ancient Greek word that translates as "the General's art". From the ancient Greek, through military to modern business usage, the word retains much of its original meaning—

- Decisions and actions with *long-term* and *wide-ranging* consequences.

- Pinpointing *vulnerabilities* in the opponent's position.

- Exploiting *resources* and *deployment* relative to opponents.

- Using *topography*, and *technology* for advantage.

For those of us who struggle every day with productivity, quality and schedules, these concepts are pretty vague. They seem irrelevant to the current tasks. As engineers, workers, specialists and managers most of us have too many and too much:

- Too Many Projects
- Too Many Priorities
- Too Many Priority Changes
- Too Many Policies
- Too Many Problems

- Too Many Mistakes
- Too Many Bosses
- Too Much Paperwork
- Too Much Criticism
- Too Much To Do

In most cases, the "Too Many and Too Much Syndrome" is traceable to an absence of strategic thinking—*not erroneous strategic thinking but absence of strategic thinking.* Strategic thinking helps the entire organization focus on a manageable set of priorities. Manufacturing Strategy ensures a match, or congruence, between the company's markets and the existing and future abilities of the production system.

Manufacturing strategy generally addresses issues including:

- Manufacturing capacity
- Production facilities
- Use of technology
- Vertical integration
- Quality

- Production planning/materials control
- Organization
- Personnel

Probably the best illustration of Manufacturing Strategy (or lack of it) is Wickham Skinner's Harvard Case study, **"The Great Nuclear Fizzle At Babcock & Wilcox."** The study describes a sea of troubles surrounding a very old, very competent builder of steam boilers in the 1960's. It includes high costs, delivery failures, technology problems, quality issues, labor troubles, lawsuits, personality conflicts and the suicide of a key manager. Skinner traces all of this to a single issue: B&W's failure to identify their **Key Manufacturing Task."** A version of this case study is available for download at the Strategos website, www.strategosinc.com. We highly recommend it.

So, how would you recognize a Manufacturing Strategy if you happened across one? It may take one or more or the following forms:

- **Corporate Policy**—A policy statement that guides decisions about programs, facilities, capital equipment, employee relations, and other topics. These statements can be quite brief, perhaps 2-6 total pages. They guide the answers to questions such as: *"Should we purchase a manual machine, hard automation or computerized, flexible automation for this operation?"*

- **Big Boss**—Some effective strategies are entirely in the minds of owners or powerful managers. They form a pattern of decisions over time. Everyone knows how the Big Boss thinks and they make decisions accordingly.

- **Corporate Culture**—A corporate culture may embed within it the company's manufacturing or operations strategy. "This is the way we do things around here."

Manufacturing Strategy at Toyota initially used the Big Boss approach where Taiichi Ohno dictated policy and demanded results. Later, Ohno's strategy became imbedded in a variety of policies and procedures and was further imbedded in the culture. Any of these forms can be effective but there are some problems with the "Big Boss" and corporate culture approaches.

The Big Boss approach is rarely suitable for large firms. Partly this is because direct influence dissipates after moving downwards more than about two levels in a hierarchy, although this depends somewhat on the Big Boss. Another reason this is ineffective in large companies is the lack of buy-in and participation. Finally, the Big

Boss can, and often is, wrong. Knowledge and experience diffused within the company does not find its way into the strategy.

Firmly established corporate cultures can be very powerful. They influence attitudes and decisions over many years or even decades. In recalling my own experience at Ford Motor Company in the 1960's, the influence of the corporate culture established by Henry Ford I, Charles Sorensen and a few others strongly prevailed twenty years after their departure. This was a serious problem at Ford because the environment had changed. Yet, the culture and Manufacturing Strategy was frozen in a 1930 time warp. I suspect that the same is true with the other American auto companies and I doubt that it has changed much to this day. This explains why Toyota, Honda, Nissan and Hyundai have been very successful building cars in the U.S. while the old-line firms flounder.

So it is that corporate culture is an important, often the most important, element of Manufacturing Strategy. Toyota itself may find their own corporate culture a liability if the environment changes again. On the other hand, a large part of Toyota's culture emphasizes change and improvement. This may carry them through some drastic changes in technology and the business environment.

For most firms a conscious, organized look at Manufacturing Strategy that culminates in a set of Manufacturing Strategy Statements is the best approach. The Big Boss may heavily influence such an effort. Eventually, it finds its way into the corporate culture. This approach taps into a broad knowledge base, generates buy-in and yet leaves the door open for future change.

List Thinking

Much of the Lean Manufacturing literature presents lean as a series of elements, tools and techniques as in table 12. This is not a complete list and there are many variations of the names for these elements.

These "Laundry Lists" often lead towards piecemeal implementation where one element is introduced, then another and then another. This is what Barry Richmond calls "List Thinking." It ignores the systemic nature of lean in which elements interact to magnify the total effect. It also supplies little guidance for prioritizing or sequencing these elements.

Lean Manufacturing Elements, Tools and Techniques

- Cellular Manufacturing
- Total Quality
- Teams
- Rapid Setup (SMED)
- Kanban
- Metrics & Measurements
- Mixed Model Production
- Value Stream Mapping
- Process Mapping
- Work Balancing
- 5S
- Autonomation
- Pokayoke
- Jidoka
- Elimination of Waste
- Total Productive Maintenance
- Continuous Flow
- One Piece Flow
- Standard Work
- Visual Management
- In Station Process Quality
- Level Production
- Takt Time
- Point of Use Storage
- Kaizen
- Supplier Development

Table 13 Elements, Tools and Techniques

Imagine a physician with a list of the top twenty drugs. He prescribes the same list to every patient, regardless of symptoms, assuming that one of them will cure the problem. This thought does not inspire confidence and the approach is unlikely to work on a complex system like the human body. Nor will it work for a factory.

"This combo works for all my patients!"

List thinking is especially problematic when implementing. All the elements in the Laundry List of table 12 have value in some situations. However, the list gives no guidance for priorities, precedence or impact. Indeed, it cannot because each factory and situation is unique. Examining this topic strategically and systemically raises several questions:

- Do we need the entire list of "Tools and Techniques?"
- If not, which do we employ?
- Which elements come first?
- Do we implement Lean Manufacturing company-wide or in focused areas?
- How does Kaizen fit into the picture?
- How detailed should the plans be?
- How long will it take?
- How do we know when we are really Lean?

Systems Thinking

Figure 58 illustrates the systemic nature of Lean Manufacturing. Each cloud represents an element or an effect. The straight arrows represent positive influence. For example, faster setups (Near the bottom of figure 58) enable and encourage smaller batches.

The shaded circular arrows in figure 58 represent reinforcing loops or "virtuous circles." While faster setups encourage smaller batches, smaller batches lead to more setups. More setups lead to improved setup skills. With improving setup skills, operators make faster setups. And, so it goes, around and around. Figure 58 shows only a few of the many reinforcing loops in Lean Manufacturing.

The systemic nature of lean presents a serious problem for implementation. Until enough elements are in place to create reinforcing loops, the system does not sustain itself.

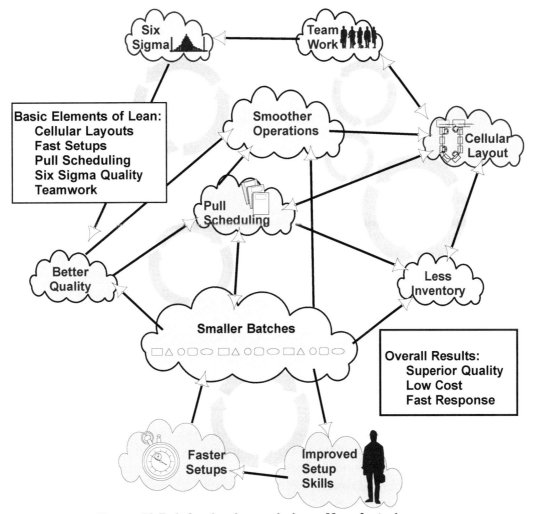

Figure 58 Reinforcing Loops in Lean Manufacturing

Socio Technical Systems & Corporate Culture

The complexity of Lean Manufacturing is actually much greater than figure 58 indicates because people are also part of this system. Figure 58 ignores most individual and group behaviors that really give lean its power. These human elements interact with each other and also with the more technical elements. It is like hardware and software—they must be designed for each other in order to work.

In the early 1950's Eric Trist and the Tavistock Institute studied the English coal mining industry where *mechanization had actually decreased productivity*. From his experience in the coalmines, Trist proposed that manufacturing (and many other) systems have both technical and human/social aspects that are tightly bound and interconnected. Moreover, it is the interconnections more than individual elements that determine system performance.

The technical system includes machinery, processes, procedures and a physical arrangement. We usually think of a factory in terms of its technical system. The social system includes people and their habitual attitudes, values, behavioral styles and relationships. It includes the reward system. It is the formal power structure as depicted on organization charts and the informal power structure deriving from knowledge and personal influence.

The social and technical systems must integrate and assist one another. For example, a manufacturing workcell that requires high teamwork will not produce in an environment of suspicion and command/control. Figure 59 illustrates.

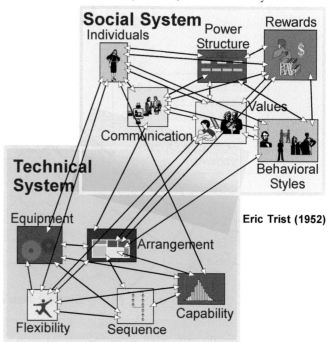

Figure 59 The Socio Technical System

When Lean Manufacturing goes awry, the root cause is often failure to appreciate its Socio-Technical and systemic nature. The socio side, in particular, is oft neglected. Team development, training and culture are just as important as fast setups and cellular layouts. Occasionally, management emphasizes teamwork and behavior and neglects the technical issues.

Example—Systemic Effects of Large Lots

Long setups and large lots illustrate one of the many reinforcing loops that exist in a conventional manufacturing system (Figure 60). There are (at least) two reinforcing loops.

In the upper loop of figure 60 large lots mean that setups are infrequent. Because setups are infrequent operators do not learn how to do them well. As with any activity, a lack of skills produces a perception that the activity is difficult and fraught with uncertainty. Such an attitude causes operators, supervisors and managers to run even larger lots in an attempt to minimize time and risk. The larger lots lead back to even fewer setups. This is like a snowball rolling downhill. The faster it goes the faster it grows and the faster it grows the faster it goes.

In the lower reinforcing loop of figure 60 large lots allow the setup cost to be amortized over more output units and apparently lowers the unit cost. This pleases the accountants and happy accountants are a relief to everyone. However, this perception also encourages even larger lots to reduce unit cost even further and the cycle goes around and around again.

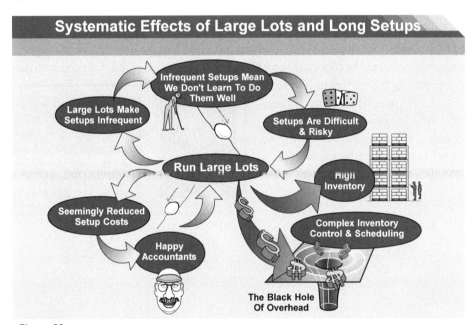

Figure 60

The end result is high inventory and a complex scheduling and inventory control system. The costs of this complex system and high inventory are mostly lost in the Black Hole of Overhead.

Lean Versus Manufacturing Strategy Approach

Wickham Skinner in his article *"Three Yards and A Cloud of Dust,"* suggested that most elements of Lean Manufacturing were like blocking and tackling in football— necessary skills but not exactly a strategy. There is some truth to this view. However, since most manufacturers do not even block and tackle very well, it is a good place to start. In this section, we ignore many of the more global elements of Manufacturing Strategy. We focus here on getting the "blocking and tackling" skills in place and operating with them in a basic system.

Toyota is the model, but only a starting model. While many elements, tools and techniques used by Toyota have broad application, they are not universal. The Toyota Production System developed at a particular time, a place and in an industry that was unique. Eiji Toyoda, Taiichi Ohno and Shigeo Shingo did not set out to develop some sort of grand, unified, and universal manufacturing theory. They simply tried to solve the specific problems that plagued Toyota in the postwar years. Different companies and industries with different products, markets and customers are likely to need different solutions, different combinations or different emphasis.

Who Should Develop Strategy?

Earlier in this chapter we suggested that the most effective form of a strategy was a set of policies that, under strong leadership, gradually insinuated themselves into the company culture. Such policies are likely to be most effective when developed in a

group setting by representatives from most parts of the firm. Many successful companies use such "Steering Committees" to formulate and then monitor strategy and implementation.

Men often oppose a thing merely because they have had no agency in planning it, or because it may have been planned by those whom they dislike.
Alexander Hamilton

5.2 Designing and Implementing Lean Manufacturing Strategy

In this section we describe how to develop strategic policies for implementing Lean Manufacturing. As mentioned before, this does not include a fundamental approach to Manufacturing Strategy but is, nevertheless, a good place to start. To develop a Lean Manufacturing Strategy and implementation plan, we recommend five general steps:

1. Evaluate The Current State
2. Identify "Key Manufacturing Task(s)."
3. Determine The Future-State Workflow (In Principle)
4. Identify Future State Infrastructure (In Principle)
5. Identify Precedents and Priorities
6. Develop The Plans

A Mental Model

While Toyota's specific solutions are not always the best for every manufacturer, the approach that developed these solutions will work anywhere. Ohno first visualized an ideal production system, in terms of workflow. Ohno's ideal system, illustrated in figure 61, was inspired by Eiji Toyoda's observations at Ford Motor Company. This ideal production system was a series of adjacent workstations that were balanced and synchronized with no inventory between stations. It delivered finished product to the customer exactly when needed (Just In Time) and drew materials, Just-In-Time. Notice the similarity of figure 61 with the ideal state process map of figure 16.

According to legend, Ohno asked Shingo and others what prevented the realization of this ultimate, no-inventory system. As the reasons surfaced, Ohno requested his deputies to "eliminate the reasons."

The resulting elements of Lean Manufacturing aim at eliminating (or at least reducing) the reasons for inventory. While the real goal is to eliminate waste, Ohno understood that inventory mirrors waste.

This thinking process is an example of what Edward DeBono calls "Lateral Thinking." By imagining an ideal, but impossible situation, we can often see more clearly, the path to its realization. First, imagine the ultimate factory as shown in figure 61 with your products and customers. Then ask the following questions:

- **What would be the characteristics of the equipment, people and layout in this factory?**
- **What must be true for this to be possible?**
- **What are the root causes for inventory in our plant?**

Figure 61 Ohno's Mental Model

Acquire Necessary Information and Experience

Training on Lean Principles

To develop a Lean strategy and implementation plan, it is necessary to know about the principles, themes, tools and techniques. In most firms, this will require some training for the Steering Committee. Steering Committee members do not all have to be lean experts but they need the basics and the advice of at least one expert. For those with essentially no knowledge, 2-3 days of training is likely to suffice for the initial strategy development. This should allow a steering committee to plan at least the initial year of implementation. Beyond this, everyone can build on basic knowledge through various means, including their own new experiences within their factory.

The Current State

The committee needs knowledge of the present state of the factory. While a Present State Value Stream Map will contain much of this information, it is seldom sufficient except in the simplest cases. Value Stream Mapping primarily addresses workflow and, to some extent, scheduling issues. It does not address a host of human and cultural issues, maintenance or quality. These also need evaluation.

Strategos' Lean Assessment tool can assist with gathering this information. The questions from this tool are in the Appendix IV. Figure 62 shows the results of a typical assessment presented as a radar chart. The largest gaps between "Target" and "Actual" should usually get the highest priorities.

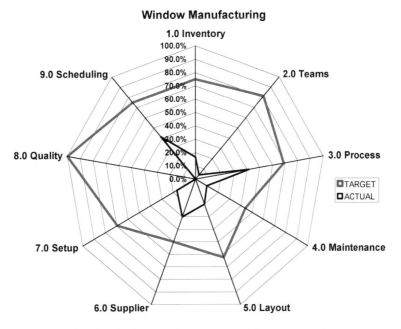

Figure 62 Typical Lean Assessment Radar Chart

Establish the Workflow

In principle, establishing the workflow is a first step. Not every detail can be worked out at this juncture but you can establish the general pattern(s). This is where mapping techniques are valuable.

Group Technology Analysis

A Group Technology analysis, in some form, is required to establish product families. In many cases this can be a very informal study using intuitive grouping. Experienced people who know the products simply divide them into Value Streams or families as discussed in Chapter 4.

More complex product-process mixes, as found in many machining or sheet metal job shops, may require a more rigorous analysis using Production Flow Analysis or Coding and Classification.

Value Stream Mapping and Process Mapping

Where only a few high-volume families exist, map each family with VSM or Process Mapping. Where there are more than about six or eight product families, map several of the more representative families. The solutions developed are likely to apply to most other product families as well.

Material Flow Diagrams

Value Stream and Process Maps give little indication of plant geography. Neither do they show the complexity of material movement that results from many overlapping value streams. Material flow diagrams as shown in figures 63 and 64 can assist in understanding this complexity.

Figure 63 is a "String Diagram." It shows material movement in situations with multiple products and multiple routings. A series of connected arrows represents the movement of an individual product. Different colors, widths or patterns for each arrow can help to differentiate the various products, although figure 63 does not use this feature.

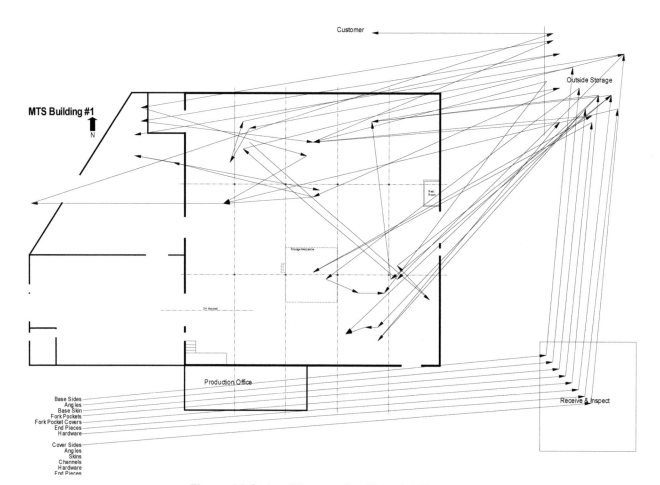

Figure 63 String Diagram for Material Flow

In figure 63, all products follow a common route from the supplier to the outdoor storage area. From that point, the paths and routes diverge. The result is a very complex material-handling situation. In the factory, such complex flows result in a complicated aisle system, many piles of parts, partially complete parts and significant inventory storage areas scattered throughout.

The "River Diagram" of figure 64 also represents material flow. It is helpful where the flow paths are simple and many items follow the same path. In this diagram, the arrow width is proportional to the magnitude of material movement.

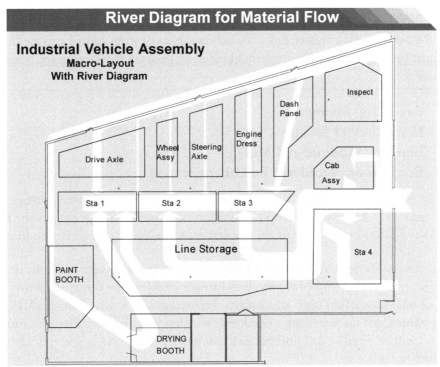

Figure 64

Select the Initial Lean Elements

Once the background information has been gathered and discussed it is time to decide what lean elements are most applicable. Later we will **set priorities** for these elements.

Most of the Lean Manufacturing literature gives lists of lean elements, tools and techniques and often detailed descriptions. There is little guidance about which are relevant in a particular situation. VSM gives some guidance with respect to workcells and kanban but not much else. The Lean Assessment can assist in pointing out deficiencies. It is up to the Steering Committee to now **match particular elements with the known deficiencies.**

Figure 65 attempts to assist with this. Areas of the Lean Assessment are in the left column of figure 65 and various elements, tools and techniques of lean are across the top. The bullets indicate that a particular element impacts the corresponding area of the Lean Assessment. The grayscale of the bullets indicate that the impact is major, minor or intermediate. To use figure 65, identify those areas of assessment with the largest gaps between "Actual" and "Target." Then move across that row to the right and determine which elements are likely to have the most impact on improving that particular area.

Figure 65 is a **very general** depiction. It attempts to show very complex interactions that are highly conditional. It is *mostly* true in *many* situations. However, every factory is somewhat different and figure 65 is an initial guide, not a substitute for analysis, common sense and deep experience.

Identify Precedents & Priorities

Once the Steering Committee has decided on the most important Lean elements, they must prioritize them for implementation. In general, the factors for deciding priorities are:

- **Cash Flow Saving**
- **Immediacy of Savings**
- **Impact on Culture and Morale**
- **Enablers or Precedents for Other Elements**

The idea is to implement first those elements that will start generating positive cash flow quickly. By doing so, the implementation becomes self-financing as the new cash flows fund other aspects of the implementation that take more time to payoff.

Precedents are somewhat different than priorities. Some elements of Lean do not immediately payoff in and of themselves but are enablers for other elements. Rapid Setup or SMED is often such an element. Here, the direct payoff from SMED may not be particularly large in itself. The benefit is that it enables smaller lots and enables kanban. Smaller lots and Kanban do payoff handsomely and quickly with inventory reductions.

Legend: Minor / Intermediate / Major

Lean Elements, Tools & Techniques

Assessment Areas — Positive Impacts / Causes------->	Cellular Manufacturing	Team Development	Kanban	Mixed Model Production	Mapping Techniques/VSM	Work Balancing	Level Production	Takt Time	Metrics & Measurements	5S	Visual Management	Jidoka	Supplier Development	Pokayoke	Total Quality/Six Sigma	Standard Work	Autonomation	Continuous Flow	Rapid Setup (SMED)	Total Productive Maintenance
1.0 Inventory	Intermediate		Intermediate	Intermediate	Intermediate		Intermediate		Minor				Intermediate						Intermediate	
2.0 Teams & Culture	Minor	Intermediate	Minor						Intermediate	Intermediate	Intermediate	Minor				Intermediate	Minor			
3.0 Process	Intermediate			Intermediate	Intermediate	Intermediate	Minor	Intermediate	Minor	Major	Major	Minor	Major		Minor	Minor	Minor	Intermediate	Intermediate	Major
4.0 Maintenance									Minor	Major	Major	Major			Major		Major			Intermediate
5.0 Layout	Intermediate			Major	Intermediate				Minor									Intermediate	Minor	
6.0 Supplier			Major		Minor		Minor	Minor	Minor	Major			Intermediate		Minor				Major	
7.0 Setup	Major	Intermediate	Major		Intermediate				Minor	Intermediate	Intermediate							Intermediate	Intermediate	Minor
8.0 Quality	Minor	Intermediate	Minor						Intermediate	Minor	Minor	Intermediate	Minor	Intermediate	Intermediate	Minor	Intermediate	Minor	Minor	Intermediate
9.0 Scheduling	Intermediate		Intermediate	Intermediate	Intermediate		Intermediate		Minor									Minor	Intermediate	Minor

Figure 65

Figure 66 shows how selected elements and their priorities might look for four separate factories. The first column for each factory shows the priority that was established. An "N/A" notation indicates that the particular element does not particularly apply. "N/A" elements are, essentially, ignored (at least for the initial implementation). In addition, some of these elements are attitudes or themes that pervade all aspects of lean and are not elements that can be directly implemented. Some other "N/A" elements are tools for implementation of other elements.

Light Assembly—Figure 66(A) shows the elements and priorities that might be appropriate for a light assembly operation. Here the primary emphasis is on layout, Cellular Manufacturing, Teams to operate the cells and a Kanban system to supply parts. Total Productive Maintenance is considered "Not Applicable" because the only maintenance is for hand tools and utilities. A world-class maintenance department is unnecessary. This does not preclude improvements in Maintenance provided that such efforts do not detract from the other elements.

	Typical Priorities for Lean Elements						
	A		**B**		**C**		**D**
PR	**Light Assembly**	PR	**Paper Mill**	PR	**Jobbing Machine Shop**	PR	**PBC Fabrication**
1	Cellular Manufacturing	1	Rapid Setup (SMED)	1	Group Technology	1	Group technology
2	Teams	2	Maintenance (TPM)	2	Cellular Manufacturing	2	Cellular Manufacturing
3	Kanban	3	Total Quality/SPC	3	Rapid Setup (SMED)	3	Rapid Setup (SMED)
4	Mixed Model Production	4	Metrics & Measurements	4	Teams	4	Teams
5	Value Stream Mapping	5	Teams	5	Kanban	5	Kanban
6	Process Mapping	6	Standard Work	6	Process Mapping	6	Process Mapping
7	Work Balancing	7	Kanban	7	Kaizen	7	Kaizen
8	Level Production	8	Process Mapping	8	Work Balancing	8	Work Balancing
9	Takt Time	9	Kaizen	9	Takt Time	9	Autonomation
10	Metrics & Measurements	10	Autonomation	10	Metrics & Measurements	10	Supplier Development
11	5S	11	5S	11	5S	11	Metrics & Measuremts
12	Visual Management	12	Visual Management	12	Pokayoke	12	5S
13	Jidoka	13	Pokayoke	13	Total Quality	13	Poyakoke
14	Supplier Development	N/A	Cellular Manufacturing	14	Standard Work	14	Total Quality
15	Pokayoke	N/A	Continuous Flow	15	Maintenance (TPM)	15	Standard Work
16	Total Quality	N/A	Elimination of Waste	16	Visual Management	16	Maintenance (TPM)
17	Standard Work	N/A	Group Technology	N/A	Autonomation	17	Visual Management
N/A	Autonomation	N/A	In Station Process Quality	N/A	Continuous Flow	N/A	Continuous Flow
N/A	Continuous Flow	N/A	Jidoka	N/A	Elimination of Waste	N/A	Elimination of Waste
N/A	Elimination of Waste	N/A	Level Production	N/A	In Station Process Quality	N/A	In Station Process Quality
N/A	Group Technology	N/A	Mixed Model Production	N/A	Jidoka	N/A	Jidoka
N/A	In Station Process Quality	N/A	One Piece Flow	N/A	Level Production	N/A	Level Production
N/A	Kaizen	N/A	Point of Use Storage	N/A	Mixed Model Production	N/A	Mixed Model Production
N/A	One Piece Flow	N/A	Supplier Development	N/A	One Piece Flow	N/A	One Piece Flor
N/A	Point of Use Storage	N/A	Takt Time	N/A	Point of Use Storage	N/A	Point of Use Storage
N/A	Rapid Setup (SMED)	N/A	Value Stream Mapping	N/A	Supplier Development	N/A	Takt Time
N/A	Maintenance (TPM)	N/A	Work Balancing	N/A	Value Stream Mapping	N/A	Value Stream Mapping

Figure 66

Paper Mill—Figure 66 (Column B) is appropriate for a paper mill. Massive and expensive paper machines dominate papermaking. A typical mill might have only 2-6 such machines that are specialized for particular grades. There is little opportunity for Cellular Manufacturing and the primary considerations are setups, Maintenance and Quality.

Jobbing Machine Shop—Operations such as a job-shop may have thousands of different products and dozens (or hundreds) of specialized machine tools. Sorting out this complex product-process mix requires Production Flow Analysis or Classification and Coding. While these GT analyses require major effort, the benefits of workcells in such situations are enormous and well worth the effort. Setup Reduction also plays a major role, as does Team Development. (Figure 66(B)

PCB Fabrication—Printed Circuit Boards (Figure 66(D)) will also require a GT analysis. However it may be less formal than typically found in a machining or sheet metal job shop. Cellular Manufacturing is important, as is setup reduction on the SMT equipment.

General Principles for Implementation

Flexibility, concentration and beachhead strategies are important general principles. They are especially relevant to an initial Lean implementation.

Strategic Flexibility

Our knowledge, at this point is incomplete. Unexpected problems arise to change any plan. However, *unforeseen opportunities* also arise. This is where master strategists excel. Field Marshal Erwin Rommel, for example, was successful in North Africa

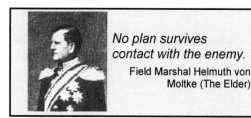

No plan survives contact with the enemy.
Field Marshal Helmuth von Moltke (The Elder)

because he often deviated from plans to take advantage of unforeseen opportunities.

The only sure thing is change. Tasks in the near future are less likely to change than tasks months away. We suggest two plans:

- **A short term, detailed, rolling plan for 3-6 months**
- **A long-term, general plan for 6-36 months.**

The long-term plan sets direction and budgets. The short-term plan tracks specific tasks, activities and accomplishment. When problems and opportunities develop, these dual plans are easy to change.

Concentration

One of Von Clauswitz' principles of war is concentration—concentrate maximum force in the minimum area and where the opposition is weakest. Business strategy has a corresponding principle for a different reason. Few individuals or organizations cope effectively with more than 2-3 high-priority objectives. As objectives multiply, efforts scatter and people flit from one task to another. Everything slows down and the work that is done is half-baked. Most importantly, new practices fail to become institutionalized.

In developing an implementation plan, ensure that no more than 2-4 major initiatives occur simultaneously. In addition, particular individuals or groups should not be heavily involved in more than one or two of these objectives. Maintenance and Engineering are the groups that most frequently become overwhelmed.

Beachhead Strategies

If we attempt to implement and migrate one initiative at a time through a large company, results take forever. It is also difficult to sustain one initiative until the next arrives to reinforce it. In addition, many forces within the organization can work against such a radical change as Lean Manufacturing.

A beachhead strategy focuses on a small area or a product. All essential elements for a self-reinforcing, sustainable system are deployed, albeit locally. This can happen quickly. The small area becomes a beachhead of Lean Manufacturing.

Others in the organization may observe and learn from the beachhead. Gradually, one product and one area at a time, the beachhead expands.

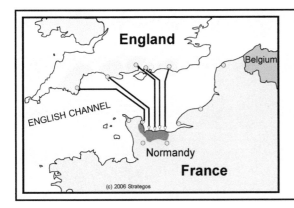

D-Day, June 6, 1944.

The Allied landing in Normandy was the largest amphibious invasion in history. Allied armies were greatly outnumbered by the Axis, particularly during the first few days. The Axis armies, however, were spread over thousands of miles of coastline.

By concentrating the invasion on five small beaches, the Allies developed local superiority. Before the Axis could focus sufficient force on the landing grounds, the Allies had established a beachhead and had landed sufficient forces to defend it.

The Kaizen Blitz

The Kaizen Event (Blitz) is a focused implementation that suits a beachhead strategy. The blitz has strong appeal. It is fast, dramatic and effective. Kaizen events can implement workcells, SMED and 5S, in targeted areas, within a week or less. However, use Kaizen Events with caution; there are significant dangers; among them are:

- Kaizen Events are tactical, not strategic.

- Kaizen requires experienced, knowledgeable and wise facilitators.

- The learning in a blitz is superficial.

Kaizen events are *localized* in time and place. They can be well-executed and still result in a factory with a confused overall layout, difficult material handling and a parochial culture. Management sometimes becomes so enamored with the hoopla of Kaizen events that they depend entirely on these events for improvement with little overall planning or strategy.

Kaizen events require ***experienced facilitators*** who often make major decisions before the event even occurs. This is necessary for the event to go smoothly because participants usually do not have the in-depth knowledge to make these decisions well. The speed and intensity of Kaizen also depends upon strong direction from a facilitator. While the participants in Kaizen events are usually amateurs, a successful event depends upon a professional-level facilitator.

Participants learn a great deal during a Kaizen event. However, because time is so limited, this learning tends to be ***experiential*** and ***superficial***. This type of learning is essential but insufficient for an overall lean strategy.

Football, War and Manufacturing Strategy

For a decade, Vince Lombardi's Power Sweep dominated pro football. The power sweep was pure Lombardi: fundamental; few frills; teamwork—"four yards and a cloud of dust," perfect for Green Bay's ball-control offense.

He told his team: *"Gentlemen, if we can make this play work, we can run the football."* The Green Bay Packers did make it work, through constant drill and practice.

"You think there's anything special about this sweep? Well, there isn't. It's as basic a play as there can be in football. We simply do it over and over and over. There can never be enough emphasis on repetition. I want my players to be able to run this sweep in their sleep. If we call the sweep twenty times, I'll expect it to work twenty times...not eighteen, not nineteen."

"... on that sideline, when the sweep starts to develop, you can hear those linebackers and defensive backs yelling, `Sweep!' `Sweep!' and almost see their eyes pop as those guards turn up-field after them... It's my number one play because it requires all eleven men to play as one to make it succeed, and that's what `team' means."

"Every team eventually arrives at a lead play. It becomes the team's bread-and-butter play, the top- priority play. It is the play that the team knows it must make go, and the one the opponents know they must stop. Continued success with the play makes for a number one play, because from that success stems your confidence..."—Vince Lombardi

Strategy is more art than science and manufacturing is certainly not football, let alone war. Nevertheless, certain central themes are woven through all strategic thinking. Successful strategies mirror these common themes:

- Identifying "Leverage Points" or "Centers of Gravity."
- Concentration of efforts on the few critical areas at any given time.
- Extraordinary competence in execution of the few critical tasks.
- Appreciation and deep knowledge of the human and social aspects.
- Charismatic, visionary leadership that brings it all together.

Finding Your Power Sweep

In most situations, 2-3 changes will have more impact than everything else in the Lean repertoire combined. Peter Senge refers to these as "Leverage Points" and Von Clauswitz called them "Centers of Gravity." All efforts should *concentrate* on these *leverage points* through training, incentives and practice.

Lombardi understood this instinctively. It is why he concentrated on a few effective plays, like the Sweep, that his team had the talent for. He then practiced until execution was perfect. Lombardi also understood teamwork and motivation. One reason he favored the Power Sweep is ***that this play both demanded and encouraged teamwork.*** Green Bay guards like Jerry Kramer and Fuzzy Thurston loved the sweep because it brought offensive guards out of their normal obscurity.

Develop the Implementation Schedule

With the elements, precedents, priorities and considerations identified, it is time to work out an action plan with tasks, assignments and costs.

Phasing

We suggest three broad phases (figure 67) for a long-term Lean Manufacturing implementation:

I. Core Disciplines

  II. Consolidation

    III. Continuous Improvement

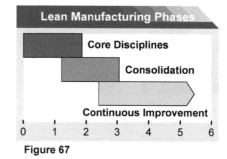

Figure 67

Phase I implements the minimum essentials for an effective system. Perhaps 60%-80% of the benefits accrue from Phase I. The changes in Phase I are dramatic, results immediate and benefits clear. When people speak of a Lean Implementation, they usually think of Phase I and Phase I is primarily our concern in this chapter.

Phase II builds on the core disciplines. It includes the later, secondary techniques. Phase II fine-tunes and improves the initial system. It includes methods and training that inculcate basic values to sustain the system.

Continuous Improvement characterizes Phase III. The improvements are many but small and incremental. Nevertheless, like compound interest, the improvements build year in and year out; phase III never ends. This is a core value at Toyota but unappreciated by most imitators.

Timeframes

The time required for Phase I varies significantly depending on the size of the firm, product-process mix, culture, leadership and other factors. Assume a "typical" factory of, say, 500 employees, 2000 or so manufactured parts, a dozen product lines, and competent leadership. For this plant, Phase I may require 3-6 months for substantial results and 12-36 months for completion. "Completion" is rather vague and the transition between Phase I and Phase II is not always clear. Phase II is evolutionary. It will probably require an additional 1-3 years.

Some firms that do well in Phase I never progress further. They are so proud of themselves that they sit down to contemplate their own greatness and never arise. The supreme wisdom of Taiichi Ohno was that he never fell victim to this.

Resource Availability

Adequate resources in time, money and people are essential to any project. In a Lean Manufacturing implementation, the availability of supporting staff is often the most critical factor. Usually this means Engineering and Maintenance. As you build the schedule try to sequence tasks in such a way that no support department has a heavy involvement in more than one or two major tasks at any given time.

Implementation Project Example

Figure 68 is a very simple example of a Phase I implementation that illustrates the principles; it anticipates three workcells. Each workcell will require Rapid Setup (SMED), kanban production control, Total Quality and Team development.

In addition, the plan anticipates a more general supplier development effort that eventually brings suppliers into the kanban system.

The Gantt chart shows a timeframe for each activity. The workcells are sequential. The more general supplier development and kanban is essentially separate. This schedule limits the number of tasks that a particular department must undertake at any one time.

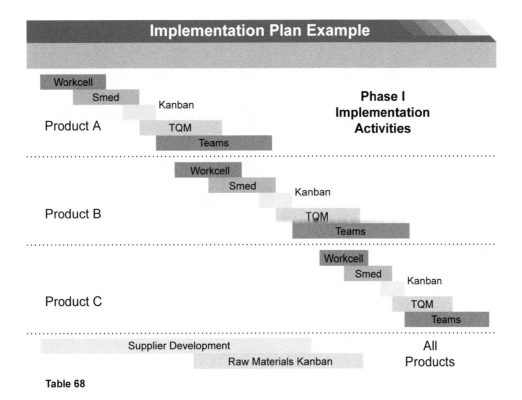

Table 68

Chapter 5 Summary

This chapter has shown how to supplement Value Stream Mapping and Process Mapping with a broader assessment of the manufacturing system. It has discussed some basics of manufacturing strategy and implementation strategy. We have discussed some of the characteristics of all strategic thinking such as the principles of Concentration and Center of Gravity.

When developing an implementation plan for Lean Manufacturing, priorities and precedents are important considerations. In addition, the other strategic principles must be incorporated in the plan. The result should be a set of project schedules for implementation. You should have a detailed short-range plan and a broader long-range plan.

Chapter

6.0 A Final Note

Simplicity is a recurring theme in engineering, manufacturing, Lean operations and, indeed, all strategic thinking. Yet, in any endeavor, it is one of the most difficult attributes to achieve.

Thus, then, in strategy everything is very simple, but not on that account very easy.
--Carl von Clauswitz

One reason for an emphasis on simple processes comes from systems theory and the science of Chaos. Simple systems are usually more stable. Complexity is one of the fundamental causes of Chaos. As most manufacturing people have experienced, chaos is endemic in many factories and is not conducive to quality, delivery reliability or low cost. Not to mention the mental health of workers and managers.

Systems theory (Ashby's Law) also tells us that simple systems require only simple controls. Thus simple manufacturing processes produce simplicity in scheduling and inventory systems and many of the other supporting systems of manufacturing.

Mapping techniques help to achieve Henry Ford's ideal of simple processes. They dramatically display complexity and point the way to simple solutions. A quick review of figures 14-19 will confirm this.

Every well – thought – out process is simple.
-Henry Ford I

Key Point Recap

- *All maps are simplified depictions of reality.* Therefore, any mapping technique shows only certain aspects of that reality while ignoring other aspects. Know several mapping techniques, choose your type of map carefully and understand its limitations.

- *The most important value of work mapping is in the process of mapping, not the final map.* Hone your facilitation skills and use maps to build understanding, generate new solutions and build consensus.

- *Mapping is not Manufacturing Strategy.* It is only a tool to assist with certain aspects of developing a comprehensive and effective Manufacturing Strategy and build a competitive position.

Appendix

7

Appendices

Appendix I—Lean Elements Tools & Techniques

Appendix II—Strategos Training Programs

Appendix III—Lean Assessment Questionnaire

Appendix IV—Balancing The Work In Workcells

Appendix I—Lean Elements Tools & Techniques

ID	Tool	Purpose	Description
1	5S	Reduce wasted time & motion at micro level.	Organized approach to housekeeping that ensures tools, parts and other objects are in known, optimum locations.
2	Autonomation	Allows automated equipment to operate without human intervention or monitoring.	Uses a wide variety of ingenious devices to monitor automated machines and stop them when problems occur. Developed at Toyota at a time when automated equipment had few devices for preventing defects or malfunctions.
3	Cellular Manufacturing	Simplify workflow and concentrate on a single product or narrow family of products. It improves quality, inventory and many other parameters.	Cellular Manufacturing organizes small work units of 3-15 people to build a single product or a narrow product family. Ideally the product is completed without leaving the workcell.
4	Continuous Flow	Coordinate production by ensuring synchronized, continuous flow throughout the value stream.	Continuous flow is the concept of moving product through a value stream at a constant rate throughout that value stream rather than in batches.
5	Continuous Improvement	To institutionalize the practice of making many small improvements every day and improve overall efficiency like compound interest.	Continuous Improvement refers to the idea that a large number of small improvements in processes are easier to implement than major improvements and have a large cumulative effect.
6	Design for Six Sigma (DFSS)	To ensure that a product's design is easy to manufacture without defects and meets customer needs.	(DFSS) applies Six Sigma principles to the design of products and their manufacturing processes.
7	Elimination of Waste	Improve efficiency and effectiveness.	Elimination of waste is an overarching theme of Lean Manufacturing. All the various tools and techniques are aimed at this ultimate goal.
8	Focused Factories	Align process capabilities with Marketing Strategy & concentrate expertise.	Segregates plants and sections within a plant by markets and product lines.
9	In-Station Quality Control	Prevents defects from passing to downstream processes and ensures immediate feedback for correction of quality problems.	Uses SPC, pokayoke and conventional inspection to ensure that products do not leave a workstation with defects.
10	Jidoka	Prevents problems on one station of a production line from building inventory or passing non-conforming work downstream. It also creates urgency to find permanent solutions.	Jidoka is the practice of stopping an integrated assembly or production line when any workstation encounters problems. Such stoppages create a crises atmosphere that encourages immediate and permanent solutions.
11	Kaizen	To improve work processes in a variety of ways.	Kaizen is a generic Japanese word for improvement or "making things better." In the context of Lean Manufacturing, it can apply to rapid improvement (Blitz) or slow continuous improvement (quick & Easy).
12	Kaizen Blitz	Improve localized production areas quickly and dramatically and overcome inertia common to many organizations.	the Blitz is an intense, highly focused improvement activity intended to redesign and implement major changes within a few days.
13	Kanban	Schedule production and minimize work-in-process while encouraging improvement in many areas.	Kanban establishes a small stockpoint (usually at the producing workcenter) that sends a signal when items are withdrawn by a downstream process. The producing workcenter simply replaces the items removed.
14	Lean Accounting	To properly account for lean activities and support the lean initiative.	Includes Activity Based Costing, process costing and other approaches that document lean savings.
15	Lean Office	Carry Lean principles to activities normally done in an office environment.	Many practices, tools and techniques of Lean Manufacturing can produce similar (or even greater) results in office and administrative environments.
16	Lean Suppliers	Push improvements upstream in the supply chain	This includes a search for lean suppliers, the development of lean in existing suppliers and a narrowing of the supplier base.
17	Mixed Model Production	Smoothes the demand on production processes upstream from a final assembly line.	This refers to Toyota's practice of building multiple models on the same assembly line simultaneously rather than in large batches.
18	One-Piece Flow	Reduce inventory internal to a workcell and forces improvements and work balance.	One-piece flow is the concept of transferring only a single piece between process steps within a workcell with no accumulation of inventory. It forces near-perfect balance and coordination.
19	Point-of-Use Storage	Reduce material movement	the practice of storing inventory at the location where it is used rather than in a warehouse or other dedicated storage facility.
20	Pokayoke	Prevent the occurrence of mistakes or defects.	Uses a wide variety of ingenious devices to prevent mistakes. An example is an automotive gasoline tank cap having an attachment that prevents the cap from being lost.

ID	Tool	Purpose	Description
21	Process Mapping	To visualize and understand the sequence and nature of events in a process at macro and micro levels.	Invented by Frank Gilbreth about 1913, process mapping visually displays Value-Added and Non-Value Added steps using only a few clear symbols and lines. It lays the foundation for and guides process improvement.
22	Production Leveling	Smoothes demand variability on processes.	Production Leveling uses various incentives to establish a steady demand rate for each product from the marketplace.
23	Pull & Synchronous Scheduling	To closely link and synchronize processes and prevent surges of WIP inventory and/or shortages.	Kanban is one method. Direct linkage of processes with conveyors or other devices is another. Broadcast scheduling in which every process in a value stream operates to the same schedule is the third principle method.
24	Quick & Easy Kaizen	Formalize, spread and maintain continuous improvement activities.	Quick & Easy Kaizen is a term originated by Norman Bodek that describes Toyota's practice of soliciting and rewarding small improvement suggestions from all employees.
25	Rapid Setup (SMED)	To minimize setup time and cost thereby freeing capacity and enabling the production of very small lots.	Rapid Setup uses Work Simplification and other conventional techniques to analyze each setup as a process and reduce time and other waste. It also tends to make setups more predictable and improve quality.
26	Self Directed Work Teams (SDWT)	SDWTs are the ultimate form teams for managing daily work.	Teams charged with managing their daily work without formal leadership.
27	Six Sigma	Improve quality, operational performance, practices and systems.	A rigorous, disciplined methodology using data and statistics.
28	Socio-Technical Systems	Improves the design of factories and offices as well as the quality of work life for individuals.	Eric Trist recognized in the early 1950's interactions between people and technology. Socio-Technical Systems theory identifies principles to optimize these interactions. Lean Manufacturing applies many of these principles.
29	Statistical Process Control	Improve quality and process capability using statistical methods.	SPC uses a variety of analysis and measuring techniques to 1) Establish that a process is capable and 2) that the process is in control (operating normally).
30	Supplier Development	Applies Lean Manufacturing principles upstream to the supplier base.	Lean Manufacturing works best with suppliers that deliver high quality components precisely when they are needed. Supplier development attempts to locate or train suppliers to do so and develop a network of competent suppliers.
31	Takt Time	To balance the output of sequential production processes and prevent inventory buildups and shortages.	The average time required between output units at a particular process coordinated with final customer requirements.
32	Team Development	To provide motivation, improved coordination, reduce management requirements and exploit the knowledge of employees.	Organizes small work groups of 5-15 people for problem solving or work management. Provides structure and interpersonal skills required for decision making.
33	Total Productive Maintenance	Ensure uptime, Improve process capability and consistency	A maintenance program that combines predictive and preventive maintenance with problem solving and Total Quality.
34	Total Quality Management (TQM)	Improve quality by preventing defects from occurring.	TQM uses a combination of SPC and problem solving teams to improve process capability and ensure that external factors do not negatively affect the process driving it out of control.
35	Value Stream Mapping	To visualize macro-level processes and their conformance to Toyota Production System (TPS) principles.	Uses a wide variety of symbols for many elements of TPS and helps determine how to employ these elements in process improvement.
36	Visual Management	To provide immediate, visual information that enables people to make correct decisions and manage their work and activities.	Visual Management uses a wide variety of signs, signals and controls to manage people and processes. Traffic signs, lights and curbs are the most familiar examples.
37	Work Balancing	To minimize idle time for people and/or equipment.	Simple technique using bar charts that helps to assign tasks to people and workstations.
38	Work Simplification	Reduce wasted time and motion at macro level	A technique that used various Industrial Engineering tools to simplify and streamline work.
39	Work Standardization	Ensure a process consistency for quality and to conduct experiements for improvement.	Organized approach to work specifications and instructions.
40	Work Standardization	To ensure that all workers execute their tasks in the same manner and thus reduce variation from differences in work method.	As practiced at Toyota, work teams carefully specify the exact manner of performing each task and then adhere to it. Changes are made by the group when that group identifies improvements.

Appendix II—Strategos Training Programs

Introduction & Principles

Lean Manufacturing Intro & Simulation	Onsite /1-Day
Lean Orientation for The Shop	Onsite / 1/2-Day
Overview of Lean	Training Kit /1-Day

Strategy

Lean Assessment	Online /Variable
Executive Leadership for Lean Manufacturing	Onsite /2-Days

Five S & Visual Control

5S & Visual Control For Work Teams	Onsite Seminar & Kaizen 1-Day
Implement & Manage 5S & Visual Control	Onsite/1-Day
5S & Visual Control For The Office	Onsite Seminar & Kaizen 1-Day
5S	Training Kit /3-Day
5S Office	Training Kit /3-Day

Human Aspects

Peak Performance Teams	Onsite/ 1-Day
Leadership In Team Environments	Onsite/ 2-Day
Executive Leadership for Lean Manufacturing	Onsite /2-Days
Creating & Sustaining A Culture For Lean	Onsite /1-Day

Facilities Planning & Workcell Design

Workcell Kaizen Event	Onsite/ 5-Day
Workcell Design	Onsite/ 2-Day
Lean Plant Layout & Facility Planning	Onsite /3-Day
Designing & Managing A Lean Warehouse	Onsite/2-Day
Warehouse & Order Picking Design	Onsite /2-3 Day

Process Improvement & VSM

Process Mapping & Value Stream Mapping	Onsite/ 2-Day Online/ 7-Wks
Value Stream Mapping	Training Kit /3-Days
Quick & Easy Kaizen	Onsite/ 1/2-Day

Lean Suppliers & Extended Value Streams

Lean Suppliers & Extended Value Stream Mapping	Onsite /3-Day

Scheduling, Inventory & Setup

Kanban System Design	Onsite/ 1-Day Online /5-Wks
Strategic Scheduling for Lean Manufacturing	Onsite/ 2-Day Online /5-Wks
Cycle Counting & Inventory Record Accuracy	Onsite /1-Day
Setup Reduction Kaizen Event (SMED)	Onsite Seminar & Kaizen 3-5 Days

Six Sigma, TQM

Introduction To Six Sigma (Call for Info)	Onsite/ 1-Day
Basic Statistical Process Control	Onsite/ 2-Day
Root Cause Analysis	Onsite /3-Day
Managerial Problem Solving	Onsite /2 Day

Accounting, Finance & Metrics

Accounting & Metrics for Lean Manufacturing	Onsite /3-Day

The Lean Office

The Lean Office	Onsite /2-Day

Appendix III—Lean Assessment Questionnaire

This assessment helps to investigate, evaluate, and measure nine key areas of manufacturing. The result is a deeper understanding of key issues, problem areas, and potential solutions. These nine key areas are:

- Inventory
- The Team Approach
- Processes
- Maintenance
- Layout & Material Handling

- Suppliers
- Setup
- Quality
- Production Control & Scheduling

The Lean Manufacturing Assessment has a questionnaire with 3-6 questions for each area and multiple-choice answers. A scoring worksheet totals the score for each section and provides an overall Lean Index.

The nine areas are not equally important in determining overall manufacturing performance. Moreover, the relative importance of the areas varies with particular products, markets, processes, and other factors. The user must evaluate the relative strategic impact of each area. This weighting feature will also help establish priorities for implementation.

For example, a firm might score very low in the area of "Maintenance". For a highly automated factory with integral processes, a low maintenance score would be a critical deficiency. For an assembly operation using hand tools and manual methods, a low ranking on "Maintenance" would have little impact.

The questions also lead to metrics for your Lean Manufacturing journey. Managers traditionally rely on accounting metrics. These are inadequate for Lean Manufacturing. Managing a lean factory requires data that reflects what is happening all along the value stream.

This format uses an Excel template to record information and score the results. It produces a "radar chart" that visually displays results. The assessment is available at the Strategos website, http://www.strategosinc.com/assessment.htm.

Inventory

Inventory is a recurring theme in Lean Manufacturing. Many authors and lecturers on Lean Manufacturing say it is "evil". Yet, inventory can serve many purposes. It allows continuous delivery while manufacturing focuses on long runs. It prevents the vagaries of maintenance and quality from interrupting schedules. It accommodates the variation of incoming orders.

Excessive inventory is not a problem nor is it evil; it is only an effect. Just as obesity and fat are not problems, only symptoms of poor diet and insufficient exercise. The fundamental causes of high inventory, like the fundamental causes of obesity lie deeper. Some of the more common causes are shown below. Notice that the various remedies, taken together, constitute the core disciplines of Lean Manufacturing.

Inventory is probably one of the two biggest assets on your company's balance sheet. It is an important determinant of Return On Assets (ROA) and other measures of financial performance. Carrying stock is expensive, usually 20%-40% of the average value per year. It devours capital-- capital the business may need for growth. It requires large warehouses and valuable floor space. It increases material handling. Large stocks require massive computer systems for tracking and control.

We usually measure inventory in "turns." Annual sales divided by average value on hand. This ratio allows comparison of larger and smaller firms. It accounts for changes in annual sales volume and seasonal fluctuation. (While there are many variations of this metric, they matter little as long as you are consistent.)

1.0	Inventory		Response	X
1.1	For the categories of Finished Goods, Work-In-Process (WIP) and Purchased/Raw Materials, what portion of middle and upper managers can state from memory the current turnover?		0%-6%	X
			7%-55%	
			56%-80%	
			81%-93%	
			94%-100%	
1.2	What is the overall inventory turnover, including Finished Goods, WIP and Purchased/Raw material?		0-3	
			4-6	
			7-12	X
			13-24	
			25+	
1.3	What is the ratio of Inventory Turnover to the industry average?		<=1.0	X
			1.1-2.0	
			2.1-4.0	
			4.1-8.0	
			8.1+	

Notes:

1.1 When management is unaware of inventory turnover, it is rarely a good thing. To answer this question, simply ask ten or so managers, selected at random. Wildly erroneous answers count as a negative response. Blank stares also count as negative.

1.2 Inventory turnover varies widely by industry but this question provides an overall benchmark.

1.3 This question compensates for industry variation by comparing turnover to an industry average. There are many sources for this industry average available for public firms. This may require some research to uncover the best industry average. A Lean company should have at least double the industry average. Very lean companies may have 10 times the industry average.

Teams and Corporate Culture

2.0	The Team Approach	Response	X
2.1	What is the organization type?	Exploitive	X
		Bureaucratic	
		Consultive	
		Participative	
		Highly Participative	
2.2	How are workers on the factory floor compensated?	Individual Incentive	
		Hourly Wage	X
		Group Incentive	
		Salary	
		Salary+Annual Bonus	
2.3	To what extent do people have job security?	Layoffs Every Year	X
		Layoffs	
		Layoffs Are Rare	
2.4	What is the annual personnel turnover	31%+	X
		14%-30%	
		7%-11%	
		3%-6%	
		0%-2%	
2.5	What percentage of personnel (ALL Personnel) have received at least eight hours of teambuilding training?	<5%	X
		6%-10%	
		11%-30%	
		31%-90%	
		91%-100%	
2.6	What percentage of personnel are active members of formal work teams, quality teams, or problem-solving teams?	<5%	X
		6%-10%	
		11%-30%	
		31%-90%	
		91%-100%	

Notes:

2.1 Participative organizations work best with Lean concepts. Exploitive organizations are unlikely to have any significant success. A survey is the best approach to this question since manager's opinions are likely to be far to optimistic. (See following page.)

2.2 Individual incentives (Piecework) do not function well in a Lean environment. Group incentives are OK when properly constructed. Various arrangements of salary, hourly and bonus arrangements are usually best.

2.4 Personnel turnover is one way to measure general satisfaction with the workplace. High turnover also results in loss of organizational learning that is necessary for Lean.

2.5 Team training is essential for workcells, process improvement, quality and many other aspects of Lean. Eight hours is a practical minimum.

2.6 Companies often train people for teams but then fail to use them effectively. This question measures the actual participation.

Organization Types

Exploitive—Exploitive organizations depend almost entirely on management and supervision for thinking, problem solving and decision-making. They use fear and money as primary motivators. Such organizations effectively handle only simple tasks requiring little communication, knowledge, cooperation or innovation. Fruit picking and the traditional garment industry are examples.

Bureaucratic—As the name implies, bureaucratic organizations are ruled by rules. Individual efforts focus on interpreting the rules rather than action to meet customer needs. Such organizations are stable in the extreme. They do not accept change quickly and respond poorly to market demands. Most defense contractors are good examples.

Consultative—Consultative organizations can effectively use many elements of JIT and WCM strategies. People will require significant training, awareness building and leadership to use all of them effectively. Implementation may be slow and difficulties will be encountered. These organizations can, on occasions, move quickly with strong leadership particularly if the action does not threaten significant power centers.

Participative—Participative organizations work well in Lean environments that require cooperation and frequent interaction. Such organizations promote individual security and trust. This allows them to experiment, change and adapt.

Process & Process Technologies

Many of these questions require considerable judgment and experience. This does not make them less real or less relevant.

3.0	Processes	Response	X
3.1	How many large-scale processes are in the plant through which 50% or more of different products must pass?	0	
		1	
		2	
		3	**X**
		4+	
3.2	How would you rate the overall bias of the plant's process selection with respect to scale?	Large Scale	
		Medium/Mixed	**X**
		Small Scale	
3.3	How easy is it to shift output when the product mix changes?	Very Difficult	**X**
		Moderately Difficult	
		Easy	
3.4	How easy is it to alter the total production rate by +/-15%?	Very Difficult	
		Moderately Difficult	**X**
		Easy	
3.5	What is management's target operating capacity?	96%-100%	
		91%-95%	**X**
		86%-90%	
		76%-85%	
		50%-75%	
3.6	How would you rate the overall bias of the plant's process selection with respect to technology level?	Complex Technologies	
		Moderate/Mixed	**X**
		Simple Technologies	

Notes:

3.1 Lean factories that make multiple products work best when each product or product group has dedicated equipment sized to the production needs of that particular product or group. When large-scale equipment is used for one or more processes and many products must pass through this equipment, significant problems in scheduling, handling, quality and changeovers result. Lean factories have, at most, one or two such processes.

3.2 Several factors in conventional manufacturing drive process decisions towards large, multi-product equipment. This question is a qualitative evaluation of how these factors have worked for past decisions.

3.3 Lean processes are flexible with respect to volume and product mix. For example, if product mix changes, a lean factory may simply move workers from some workcells into other workcells.

3.4 This applies to the factory as a whole and the supply chain.

3.5 Lean factories typically have reserve capacity for most equipment. This reduces WIP and improves flexibility. An overall target of about 75% is usually quite good. Some equipment may operate at much higher rates.

3.6 Simple technologies often work best in a Lean environment. However, this is not always the case.

Maintenance

Maintenance is only critical for Lean Manufacturing when the process is heavily dependent on equipment. When most operations are manual, sophisticated maintenance techniques and high performance may bring li9ttle benefit. This should be reflected in the Strategic Impact Factor selected for maintenance.

4.0	Maintenance	Response	X
4.1	Describe equipment records and data. Include records of uptime, repair history, and spare parts. Include repair and parts manuals.	Non-Existent	X
		Substantially Complete	
		Complete & Accurate	
4.2	Excluding new installations and construction projects, what percentage of maintenance time is unplanned, unexpected, or emergency?	71%-90%	
		51%-70%	X
		26%-50%	
		11%-25%	
		0%-10%	
4.3	Does maintenance have and follow a defined preventive schedule?	No PM	
		1%-10% Coverage	X
		11%-30% Coverage	
		31%-90% Coverage	
		91%+ Coverage	
4.4	Do equipment breakdowns limit or interrupt production?	Often	X
		Occasionally	
		Frequently	
4.5	What is the overall average availability of plant equipment?	Unknown	X
		0%-75%	
		76%-90%	
		91%-95%	
		96%-100%	

Notes:

4.1 Accurate records and complete manuals are an essential for effective maintenance.

4.2 The proportion of unpredictable activity is a good measure of preventive maintenance effectiveness. This question provides a benchmark.

4.3 Preventive maintenance is essential to prevent production interruptions. It simplifies scheduling, improves quality and, overall, is less expensive that simply fixing things that break.

4.4 To answer this question, interview several production supervisors.

4.5 Availability is the portion of time that equipment is ready to operate compared to the scheduled work hours.

Plant Layout & Material Handling

An inappropriate Layout and the resultant material handling can create extraordinary difficulty and significant waste. Layout also reflects the effectiveness of other factors such as purchasing and scheduling policy.

5.0	Layout & Handling	Response	X
5.1	What portion of total space is used for storage and material handling?	71%-100%	
		46%70%	X
		30%-45%	
		16%-30%	
		0%-15%	
5.2	What portion of the plant space is organized by function or process type?	71%-100%	X
		46%70%	
		30%-45%	
		16%-30%	
		0%-15%	
5.3	How would you characterize material movement?	Pallet-size (or larger) loads, long distances (>100'),complex flow patterns, confusion, & lost material	X
		Mostly tote-size loads, bus-route transport, & intermediate distances	
		Tote-size or smaller loads, short distances (<25'), simple & direct flow pattern	
5.4	How would you rate overall housekeeping and appearance of the plant?	Messy, Filthy, Confused	
			X
		Some dirt, Occasional Mess	
		Spotless , Neat, & Tidy	
5.5	How well could a stranger walking through your plant identify the processes and their sequence?	Impossible to see any logic or flow sequence.	
		Most processes are apparent with some study. Most sequences are visible.	X
		Processes and their sequences are immediately visible.	

Notes:

5.1 Lean layouts have a high degree of Product Focus and the result is low inventory and reduced material handling. Lean factories also use scheduling and purchasing policies that contribute to low inventories. The amount of space devoted to inventory and handling reflects the effects of these strategic decisions and policies.

5.2 Process focused layouts create significant waste and are problematic in many ways. They create the need for large inventories and complex handling. This affects quality, teamwork, supervision and flexibility. This question attempts to gauge the degree of Process versus product focus.

5.3 Lean factories have relatively steady material flows—small quantities moved frequently. This question attempts to characterize that flow.

5.4 Housekeeping reflects organization at the micro level. It is also an indicator of morale and training.

5.5 This question reflects the simplicity of layout and process design. It also reflects the degree to which the factory has used Visual Control.

Suppliers are critical for complex products that cannot be completely built under one roof. A lean Supply Chain uses dependable suppliers in long-term relationships. It is built on trust and past performance. A Lean Supply Chain also requires frequent deliveries in correct amounts with high quality.

6.0	Suppliers	Response	X
6.1	What is the average number of suppliers for each raw material or purchased item?	2.5+	
		1.6-2.4	
		1.3-1.7	**X**
		1.2-1.4	
		1.0-1.1	
6.2	On average, how often, in months, are items put up for re-sourcing?	1-11	
		12-17	
		18-23	
		24-36	**X**
		36+	
6.3	What portion of raw material & purchased parts come from qualified suppliers with no need for incoming inspection?	0%	**X**
		1%-10%	
		11%-30%	
		31%-70%	
		70%-100%	
6.4	What portion of raw material and purchased items is delivered directly to the point of use without incoming inspection or storage?	0%	**X**
		1%-10%	
		11%-30%	
		31%-70%	
		70%-100%	
6.5	What portion of raw materials and purchased parts is delivered more than once per week?	0%	
		1%-10%	**X**
		11%-30%	
		31%-70%	
		70%-100%	

Notes:

6.1 Multiple suppliers for each part indicate a lack of trust that is probably based on poor past performance.

6.2 Frequent re-sourcing of items indicates that suppliers cannot be trusted to deliver at a competitive price. It also detracts from the Purchasing Department's ability to pay attention to individual suppliers and work towards a more open and trusting relationship.

6.3 This question is an indicator of supplier quality.

6.4 Direct delivery to point of use reduces waste by bypassing the usual receiving, inspection and transport steps. It requires streamlined purchasing and receiving processes and trusted suppliers.

6.5 This question measures the ability of current suppliers to deliver in frequent, small quantities. Not all factories require this for all parts. Apply judgment here.

Fast setups allow smaller lots and enhance scheduling flexibility. They allow faster replenishment and smooth the flow for kanban. Setup may also apply to manual operations where fixtures, parts and people may require time to changeover from one product to another. With some processes, setup is a minor consideration and this should be reflected in the Strategic Impact Factor.

7.0	Setups	Response	X
7.1	What is the average overall setup time (in minutes) for major equipment?	61+	
		29-60	
		16-30	X
		10-15	
		0-9	
7.2	What portion of machine operators have had formal training in Rapid Setup techniques?	0%	X
		1%-6%	
		7%-18%	
		19%-42%	
		43%-100%	
7.3	To what extent are managers and workers measured and judged on setup performance?	Not at All	X
		Informal Tracking & Review	
		Setup Tracked, Performance In Job Description	

Notes:

7.1 This question examines and benchmarks overall, average setup times on major equipment. This is an approximate benchmark and interpretation requires some judgment. However, setups of more than 0.5 hours are usually problematic.

7.2 This question applies only to operators of equipment that requires significant setup. It intends to capture the effort that has gone into setup reduction.

7.3 Few manufacturers track setup performance and evaluate the results. This is necessary to maintain good setup performance.

Of course, high quality is a prerequisite for any manufacturer today. However, the way that quality is achieved has a large effect on productivity and overall effectiveness. This section emphasizes Statistical Process Control (SPC). SPC may be unnecessary when the process itself has high stability and is inherently capable. In most cases, however, SPC is vital even for manual operations and where quality is not easily measured.

8.0	Quality	Response	X
8.1	What portion of manufacturing employees have had basic SPC training?	0%-6%	X
		7%-55%	
		56%-80%	
		81%-93%	
		94%-100%	
8.2	What portion of operations are controlled with Statistical Process Control (SPC)	0%	X
		1%-10%	
		11%-30%	
		31%-70%	
		71%-100%	
8.3	What portion of the SPC that is done is accomplished by operators as opposed to Quality or Engineering specialists?	0%	X
		1%-10%	
		11%-30%	
		31%-70%	
		71%-100%	
8.4	What is the overall defect rate?	19%+	X
		10%-18%	
		5%-9%	
		2%-4%	
		0%-1%	

Notes:

8.1 Universal SPC training is an important step in any quality program.

8.2 Often, SPC is emphasized but not effectively deployed. This question helps determine if it is part of daily practice and operations.

8.4 Captures and benchmarks the overall defect rate across all processes. Use this question with some judgment.

8.3 For effectiveness, SPC should be used by operators in real time. It is not uncommon to see it deployed by specialists in the front office. The results emerge days or weeks after the fact and are little more than historical documents.

Scheduling & production control systems often create many problems. They may also reflect the problems created by other policies and decisions. The best systems for Lean Manufacturing are simple and give very fast response to changes in demand. Examples are Kanban and Broadcast. MRP and ERP systems rarely work well (in general) and only work in a Lean Environment where they have been modified and supplemented with other methodologies.

9.0	Scheduling/Control	Response	X
9.1	What portion of work-in-process flows directly from one operation to the next without intermediate storage?	0%	
		1%-10%	X
		11%-35%	
		36%-85%	
		86%-100%	
9.2	What portion of work-in-process is under Kanban or Broadcast control	0%	
		1%-10%	
		11%-35%	X
		36%-85%	
		86%-100%	
9.3	What is the on-time delivery performance?	0%-50%	
		51%-70%	
		71%-80%	X
		81%-95%	
		95%-100%	

Notes:

9.1 This question, in many ways, reflects the layout and process design. Intermediate storages indicate unbalanced processes and functional layouts.

9.2 Kanban and Broadcast are the preferred scheduling methods for lean manufacturing; especially with respect to WIP.

9.3 This question measures and benchmarks on-time delivery performance.

The scheduling system plays a role in delivery performance it is not the only factor rarely the principle factor. Be cautious about assuming that failure to make schedule demonstrates scheduling problems.

Appendix IV—Balancing the Work In Workcells

Balancing a work cell is really the question of how much capacity to provide at each station or operation. This, in turn, relates to overall capacity of the cell. Decisions on workstation and overall capacity intertwine with many other factors of the cell design.

Static and Dynamic Balance

Cell designers should consider two types of balance: static and dynamic. For example, suppose a cell has six workstations. Over a period of several days or weeks, the average work time at each station is identical. This is static balance.

Static balance refers to long-term differences in capacity over a period of several hours or longer. Static imbalance results in underutilization of certain workstations, machines or people.

However, for shorter periods of hours or minutes the work times may vary significantly due to differences in product mix or natural variation in processing. This is dynamic imbalance.

Dynamic imbalance arises from either of two sources: product mix changes and variations in work time unrelated to product mix. Such imbalances are short term and occur over periods of minutes or hours.

Balancing People and Equipment

Historically, workstations have been viewed as single entities, even when comprised of several resources such as machines and people. When people have specific machine assignments, this simplification is acceptable. Work cells, however, often gain much of their productivity from separating the resources. One person, for example, may operate several machines. Here we should consider the balance of each resource separately.

Internal balance refers to balancing resources within the work cell. External balance refers to balancing the work cell with respect to external demands and supplies. External balance is frequently thought of as work cell capacity.

Balancing Equipment

In balancing equipment, we attempt to ensure that each piece of equipment in the work cell has the same amount of work. Frequently we also attempt to maximize the utilization of all equipment. Such balancing and high utilization is often counterproductive. The desire to achieve balance and high utilization comes from several sources: Accounting systems place high value on capital investment. They therefore discourage the acquisition of additional equipment if existing equipment is under-utilized. Second, the model of Henry Ford's assembly line stressed balance as a primary goal.

The Ford model was right for its time and product. It is, often, inappropriate for the varied product mix faced by today's manufacturers. Ford production used only one of several balance methods, inherent balance.

High utilization may be the wrong goal. High utilization is usually accompanied by high inventory and poor delivery performance. Figure 72 illustrates the relationship between these two parameters for a wide variety of manufacturing situations. When fast, reliable delivery brings a premium price, high equipment utilization may actually work against the firm's long-term strategic goals.

Inherent Balance

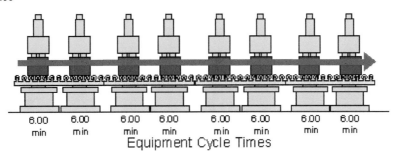

Figure 69 Inherent Equipment Balance

Inherent balance attempts to provide each workstation with precisely the same amount of work. With high-volume assembly lines this may be achievable, to some degree. Manual assembly is flexible because people are flexible. Analysts divide the work into minute tasks. They reassign these tasks to work stations such that each station has the same cycle time. Balancing mechanized or automated production lines with this method is more difficult since it is rarely possible to find equipment with identical cycle times. Figure 69 shows inherent equipment balance.

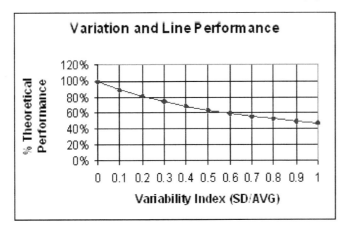

Inherent balance presents additional difficulties as well. It tends to be inflexible. For new products, the line must be re-configured and re-balanced. When multiple products run on an inherently balanced line and require differing cycle times at some operations, the line must be stopped and re-balanced at each changeover. This forces batch production.

Figure 70 Variation & Line Performance

Perhaps the most formidable problem of inherent balance comes from variation from one cycle to the next. The work times developed by traditional time study show average deterministic times of great accuracy. In reality, these times may vary significantly from one cycle to the next. The time at a given station is, in fact, a distribution. When the time on a station is longer than the average, it slows the entire line. When the time on a given station on a particular cycle is less than average, it cannot speed up the line. Thus, the real performance is less than the average cycle times indicate. The more stations, the more this variation affects performance.

Figure 71 shows the output of a simple production line at various levels of work time variation. On average, the stations are perfectly balanced at a 1.0 minutes cycle time. This line has 10 stations without queuing between stations. It shows that production output falls significantly with increased variation.

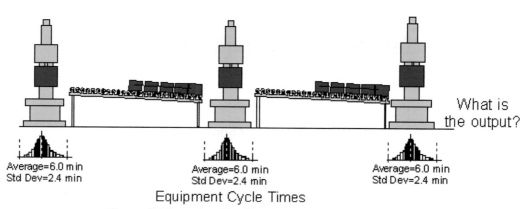

Average=6.0 min
Std Dev=2.4 min   Average=6.0 min
                         Std Dev=2.4 min   Average=6.0 min
                                                  Std Dev=2.4 min

Equipment Cycle Times
Figure 71 Queuing For Equipment Balance

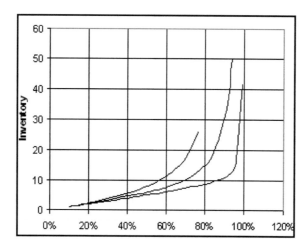

Queuing

Allowing queues between workstations is one approach that alleviates the variation problem in an inherently balanced system. Figure 71 illustrates. Here, the small queues between operations buffer small variations in cycle-to-cycle work time. Queuing does increase inventory as shown in figure 72.

Figure 72 Inventory in a Queued System

Each curve in figure 71 represents a different value of the standard deviation at the workstations. As workstation utilization increases, the inventory increases. The increase is linear and moderate at low utilizations. At higher utilization the inventory level rises dramatically. With very large variations in work time, the system chokes itself at low utilization rates.

Surplus Capacity

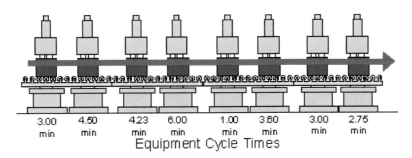

| 3.00 min | 4.50 min | 4.23 min | 6.00 min | 1.00 min | 3.60 min | 3.00 min | 2.75 min |

Equipment Cycle Times

Figure 73 Surplus Machine Capacity

The most common and, also, the most effective method provides surplus capacity for most workstations. A cell with surplus capacity at many stations is only constrained by the slowest operation, the bottleneck. Moreover, it may operate with far less internal inventory than a cell that has balanced work times. In effect, excess capacity is the tradeoff for reduced inventory and faster throughput. In figure 73, all machines but one have surplus capacity.

Balancing People

Balancing people within the cell is usually more important than balancing equipment. In most situations, the hourly cost for a person is far greater than the hourly cost for a machine or workstation. Moreover, when the workload among cell operators varies, it causes dissension in the cell team.

The methods for balancing people differ from equipment balance methods. This is because people are more flexible. They can move from one position to another. They often can perform more than a single prescribed job. They can communicate and autonomously shift to where their skills are needed.

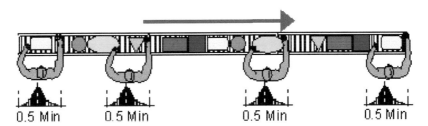

| 0.5 Min | 0.5 Min | 0.5 Min | 0.5 Min |

Figure 74 Inherent People Balance

Figure 74 shows a line that is inherently balanced. In this figure, the average work times are identical for every station and the standard deviation from cycle to cycle is quite small. This is the classical way to balance a line but difficult to achieve.

Surplus People Capacity

While surplus capacity is a reasonable method for balancing machines, particularly inexpensive machines, it rarely is acceptable for balancing people. When customer delivery is critical and customer demand irregular, surplus capacity may be used to ensure fast delivery. In figure 75, one of the six operators requires more work than any of the others. This is the bottleneck. Other operators have surplus capacity.

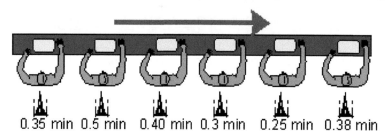

0.35 min   0.5 min   0.40 min   0.3 min   0.25 min   0.38 min

Figure 75 Surplus People Capacity

Queuing

When operators have permanent stations in a cell or line, queuing between them compensates for cycle-to-cycle variation. Floating-fixture assembly lines work on this principle. If the average work times differ, queuing alone is insufficient. Queuing alone balances the short-term or dynamic variations but it will not compensate for longer-term static variation. Figure 76 shows how these small queues buffer short-term variation. The size of the queues relates to the amount of variation. From Theory of Constraints, we know that by observing the queues, we can see which operators are most imbalanced.

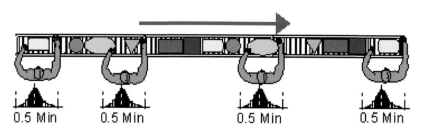

0.5 Min   0.5 Min   0.5 Min   0.5 Min

Figure 76 Queuing for People Balance

Floating

Floating balance, usually combined with queuing, is frequently a good method for balancing people. Here, operators monitor the queues to determine which stations are working ahead and which are falling behind. Operators move to the stations that are falling behind and assist until that station is caught up. This requires that stations allow for multiple operators when necessary. Figure 77 shows how operators shift position in a floating balance cell. The queues are their guide for this shifting.

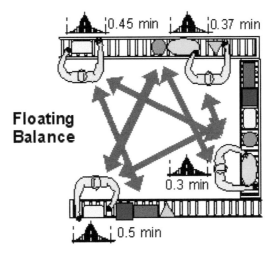

Figure 77 Floating People Balance

Circulation

With circulation, an operator carries the workpiece through all operations in sequence. This method is very flexible and perfectly balances operations. It requires that operators be completely cross-trained. It also requires surplus equipment capacity on most or all stations. Figure 78 illustrates.

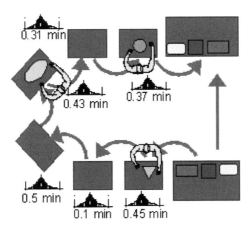

Figure 78 Circulation Balance

Summary

- Balancing work cells goes beyond traditional concepts that govern assembly line balance. Here are some of the main points from this paper:

- The issue of balance ties into larger issue of cell capacity: how much output do we need? How much capacity should each station have?

- Within a work cell, equipment and people balance are separate issues. This results from the differing characteristics of people and equipment.

- Several methods are available for balancing equipment.

- Other methods are available for balancing people.

- Hybrid approaches are also available.

Selecting an appropriate set of balancing mechanisms is one part of the cell design. Work cells are complex, subtle, and delicate socio-technical systems. The selection of balance methods must link with many other elements in the workcell design.

About The Author

Quarterman Lee has been a trusted advisor to business and industrial clients for more than 30 years. Since his first Plant Layout at Ford Motor Company in 1964, he has designed factories in many industries, including automobile, paper, electronics, printing, warehousing, plastics, foundry, metalworking and assembly.

In 1982, he traveled to Japan to observe firsthand the Toyota Production System at Toyota City and other Japanese factories. Immediately recognizing the simplicity and systemic beauty of the system, he has endeavored to adapt it to other industries and cultures.

Mr. Lee has authored more than 200 articles, books, papers and training programs on Manufacturing Strategy, Facility Planning, Plant Layout, Group Technology, Lean Manufacturing and related topics. He has taught and consulted throughout the U.S. and in China, Mexico, Ireland, Canada, Singapore, Australia and Trinidad.

Mr. Lee resides in Kansas City, Missouri, USA. He holds a B.S. in Mechanical Engineering from Purdue University.

Additional Products from Enna

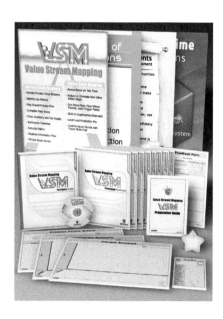

Value Stream Mapping Solution Package

Enna's Value Stream Mapping Solution Package provides all the information, materials and techniques needed to effectively lead your own Value Stream Mapping Program. It contains three full days of activities, and is structured around a teach-do format. This allows the scope of analysis to be large enough to develop a comprehensive improvement plan.

Code: 15

Value Stream Mapping Office Workflow

The VSM Office Workflow Solution is action-oriented and guides the participants through a process of analyzing the company with the Value Stream Mapping Tools.

It contains three full days of activities, and is structured around a teach-do format. This allows the scope of analysis to be large enough to develop a comprehensive improvement plan. The Facilitator is provided with information on preparing for the office environment event.

Code: 16

Additional Products from Enna

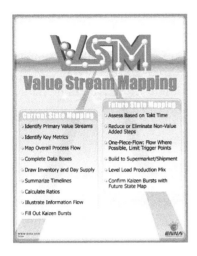

VSM Poster

This poster supports Enna's Value Stream Mapping Program and is a great overview of the steps of Value Stream Mapping. It is a great visual tool to promote continuous improvement in your organization. Use this poster during your VSM workshops and afterwards to make change more enjoyable for all involved.

Code: 76

VSM: Kaizen Bursts

These Kaizen Bursts use 3M Post-it Note adhesive to stick to most surfaces; use them to capture improvement ideas while developing your current and future state maps or other brainstorming exercises.

Code: 103

VSM: Data Boxes

These Data Boxes use 3M Post-it Note adhesive to stick to most surfaces and are perfect for capturing your value stream data. Use them as the basis for all collection of data in order to standardize information gathering and keep the user focused on accurate collection.

Code: 102

Additional Products from Enna

5S Solution Package

The 5S Solution Package will help you develop an exceptional Factory 5S program in a shop floor environment that puts your shop floor improvement activity ahead of the competition. Whether it is a Kaizen Blitz, TPM or SMED Quick Changeover, success or failure of an improvement initiative can be traced to the robustness of your 5S program.

Code: 12

5S Office Solution Package

The 5S Office Solution Package will help you develop an exceptional 5S office kaizen program in an office environment that puts your organizational development ahead of your competition.

Code: 13

Overview of Lean Solution Package

By communicating the fundamental elements of Lean Manufacturing and the history of Lean your people will understand why change is necessary and how they can assist in the change process.

Code: 11

SMED - Quick Changeover Solution Package

Enna's SMED Quick Changeover Solution Package provides all the information, materials, and techniques needed to effectively lead your own SMED Quick Changeover Program.

Code: 14

Quick & Easy Kaizen Solution Package

The experience of the God Father of Lean manufacturing, Norman Bodek, is now available in a training package. Quick and Easy Kaizen is the most effective and powerful way to implement a practical and sustainable employee-led improvement system by encompassing the often-ignored, human (employee) side of Lean manufacturing.

Code: 18

Index

B

Barnes, Ralph, 14
Beachhead Strategies
  D-Day, 123
Berra, Yogi, 25
Big Boss approach, 107, 108
brainstorming, 29, 31, 43, 68
Broadcast System, 71
bureaucratic organizations, 139

C

Calculating Inventory
  Little's Law, 62
calculating work times, 61
Cellular Manufacturing, 88
Chaos, 129
Coding & Classification, 101, 102, 103,
  104
Columbo approach, 29, 30, 43, 68
Conducting the Future State Meeting, 43
Conducting the Present State Meeting, 41
Consultative organizations, 139
corporate culture, 107, 108
Corporate Culture, 111
cost reduction, 10
Current State Map, 74
customer, 15, 19, 22, 36, 37, 38, 46, 53, 58,
  68, 71, 81, 85, 87, 92, 95, 97, 114, 139,
  152
Customers, 15, 92
cycle (process) time, 62

D

data box, 8, 58, 61
Develop the Implementation Schedule,
  126

E

Exploitive organizations, 139
extended value stream maps, 76

F

Facilitating
  future state maps, 74
  leverage points, 45
  process mapping sessions, 40
  value stream mapping sessions, 73
FIFO processes, 71
FIFO systems, 64
Five-S, 75

G

Gantt chart, 127
General Principles for Implementation,
  122
Gilbreth, Frank, 9
Group Technology, 23, 47, 48, 75, 76
Group Technology Analysis, 117

H

Hamilton, Alexander, 113
histogram, 28, 31, 42, 43

I

Information, 18
Input Lines, 18
Intuitive grouping, 101, 102
inventory control, 14, 63, 92, 112
Ishikawa Diagram, 45

K

Kaizen bursts, 73
kaizen event, 17, 101, 123, 124, 134, 135
Kaizen event, 124
Kaizen events, 123
kanban, 14, 39, 44, 49, 63, 69, 71, 72, 73,
  79, 92, 95, 99, 119, 120, 127, 145
Kanban scheduling, 92, 93
kanban stockpoint., 39, 72
Kanban systems, 71
Key Manufacturing Task, 107

T - #0313 - 160425 - C165 - 279/216/8 - PB - 9781897363430 - Gloss Lamination